Positioning Yoursel
Supernatural Power, Provision, and Protection

MW01049571

the

Will of God

the Key to Your Success

RICK RENNER

The Will of God — The Key to Your Success:
Positioning Yourself To Live in God's Supernatural Power,
Provision, and Protection

ISBN: 978-168031254-6
Copyright © 2019 by Rick Renner
1814 W. Tacoma St.
Broken Arrow, OK 74012

Published by Harrison House Publishers
Shippensburg, PA 17257
www.harrisonhouse.com

8 9 10 11 12 / 26 25 24 23 22
8th Printing

Editorial Consultants: Cynthia D. Hansen and Rebecca L. Gilbert
Text Design: Lisa Simpson, www.SimpsonProductions.net

DEDICATION

This book is dedicated to the amazing team that God supernaturally assembled to serve alongside Denise and me and our family. I am filled with thankfulness that He has blessed me with the gift of serving in this wonderful ministry with people of your caliber. God has given me many honors, but one of the greatest honors He has ever given me is the opportunity to advance the work of His Kingdom together with you. I love each of you dearly and am so thankful for you. As we keep our gaze fixed on the Lord and serve Him with humility, we can be assured that He will direct our steps in His will and continually lead us on paths of righteousness.

CONTENTS

PREFACE

Over many years of ministering to people, I've become aware that people all over the world long to know God's will for their lives. That has certainly been true of me, especially when I was younger. I longed fervently to know exactly which path God wanted me to take for my life.

The reason I refer to this as an earlier season in my life is that today I generally know God's plan for me. However, I vividly remember trying to hear His voice in my younger days so I could understand what He wanted me to do. Once I began to get a glimpse of God's plan for my life, I endeavored to gain greater understanding on *how* to do what He had revealed to me. I ardently followed the Holy Spirit's leading to the best of my ability as I launched into what I believed God had spoken to my heart.

When I finally understood the general purpose God had called me to fulfill — and exactly what kind of gifts and calling He had assigned to me — that understanding provided guidance for the rest of my life. From that time to the present, I've been living in accordance with what the Lord revealed to me at that younger age. Certainly as time has passed, the assignment has changed, adapted, and grown. That is not surprising. Jesus said if we are faithful over little, He will give us more (*see* Matthew 25:21). Anyone who has been diligent will find that his or her assignments enlarge over the years.

Knowing my purpose provided clarity to my life. I understood what I was to do — and what I was *not* supposed to do. My knowledge of His will for my life made it easier to know what to say yes to and what to say no to. It helped me know how to plan my schedule, finances, and other resources to make sure I was on track with what had been assigned to me. And this has held true through the years to the present day. I've lived with just one goal in my life: to do exactly what God asks me to do. I long to hear Jesus say, "Well done, thou good and faithful servant."

What God asked me to do is different than what He has asked others to do. At first, as a younger man, I compared myself to others and often judged myself for being different. I knew that my thought process and my approach to the Bible were different. Even my style of Bible teaching seemed to be different than others. As the years passed, I eventually understood that being different gave distinction to my life — carving out a niche that was uniquely mine — and that I didn't need to be ashamed, feel inferior, or conclude that I was odd.

As I embraced the place in God's plan that He had assigned to me, I began to enjoy it and to actually flourish in it. It took me awhile to really come into alignment in my thinking regarding who God had made me to be. But when I did pass out of that miserable stage of comparing myself to others and finally accepted what God had called me to do in life, I began to appreciate and value the gifts He had imparted to me. At that point, everything changed.

Along the way over these years, I have occasionally gotten off track — and I discuss those moments candidly in this book.

Maybe you have veered off course from what God has asked you to do as well. If that is true of you, this is a great opportunity to repent and get back on course. You'll see from my testimony in the following pages that even if you did accidentally deviate from God's path, you can get back on track relatively quickly and position yourself in the place God designed for you.

If "off course" is an apt description of your present season, it's likely that you've been experiencing some frustration. But once you get back in the center of God's will, you'll find that frustration will leave and His covenant blessings will begin working mightily in your life.

That is actually the purpose of this book — to help you not only discover God's plan, but also fully align yourself with the purpose He has designed for your life. These are the necessary steps that will move you into the ongoing experience of His supernatural *power, provision, and protection* that is so critical to fulfill your assignment.

In this book, I use the example of the apostle Paul's spiritual journey as a foundational example to show you how to avoid or overcome misjudgments and bumps that can occur along the way to your God-designed destination. My view of Paul's ministry may be unique compared to what you have heard before. But my prayer is that as you read this book with an open mind, you will learn from the points I present in these pages. My respect for the apostle Paul is enormous — so great, in fact, that I've devoted a majority of my adult life studying Paul, his epistles, and his life. What I have learned of him and his story has provided strength and encouragement for me in my own journey.

I pray that this book is a blessing to you. If it is, please think about giving a copy to a fellow traveler who is en route to finding and walking out God's plan — and is trying to learn how to do it *right*. It is my fervent prayer that this book will encourage you and others who read it.

Rick Renner
Moscow, Russia
December 2018

Teach me your decrees, O Lord;
I will keep them to the end.
Give me understanding
and I will obey your instructions;
I will put them into practice with all my heart.
Make me walk along the path of your commands,
for that is where my happiness is found.

— Psalm 119:33-35 *NLT*

CHAPTER ONE

THE SURPRISING CALL OF GOD

*I*f you are seeking to know the will of God for your life, I believe you have picked up a book that you will find very helpful in your journey of faith. It is important to understand that *knowing* the will of God and actually being *in* it are two very different things. Many know God's will, but they struggle to comply with what He has revealed about the path He has ordained for them to walk in.

Often, even if a person fully understands what God is asking, it takes time to mentally adjust to what He has revealed. I know this has been true in my life, over and over again, and it has been true in the lives of many respected leaders I know.

Even those who have given it their very best have made mistakes along the way as they've sought to fulfill God's will. The problem is not God; the problem is His children's lack of understanding or their mistakes in following His plan.

As you study the Bible, you will find that nearly everyone who heard God speak to them and reveal a special plan He had for their lives experienced bumps along the way. Those bumps were often a consequence of incomplete obedience, a misunderstanding regarding God's instructions, or simply a struggle with embracing what He had asked them to do. But the good news is this: God is willing to work with anyone who has a heart to keep trying!

As you read the pages that follow, you will find the stories of a few key biblical characters who heard God's call yet struggled to fully embrace it. You'll see that it was when they finally did fully embrace their divine assignment that they experienced miraculous and powerful results.

> **As you study the Bible, you will find that nearly everyone who heard God speak to them and reveal a special plan He had for their lives experienced bumps along the way.**

We will primarily study the life story of the apostle Paul and the journey he walked to fully embrace God's call on his life to become "the apostle of the Gentiles" (Romans 11:13). In these pages, I share a rather different view than many, gleaned from my studies of the book of Acts. We'll explore Paul's inward struggle to accept God's call to become the apostle to a people who were not his preferred choice. You will read of the obstacles he experienced along the way to fully step into that calling and what finally happened when he wholly transitioned into the plan God had prescribed for his life. It is a remarkable journey of faith!

My respect for the apostle Paul is enormous, and I have devoted much of my adult life to studying his epistles and his example. He wrote much of the New Testament, and his ministry helped shape Early Church history. Besides Jesus, no one has impacted me more than the apostle Paul, and his letters and writings have shaped my entire life. God chose this remarkable man to write much of the New Testament Scriptures, and through his Spirit-inspired epistles, Paul is still speaking to us today. In fact, I know of no better example of a man who was wholly devoted to the purposes of God.

But as I've studied Paul's life story, I've also found great encouragement in realizing that even he had to come to a place of complete surrender to God's plan for his life. If that was true of Paul, don't be surprised if it is true of you too!

Paul was one of the most unlikely candidates you could ever imagine to be called by God into the ministry. In fact, I'm going to show you that if God was able to use Paul, He can use anyone! And even if you don't see this truth at the moment, I assure you that this "anyone" includes *you*.

In the following pages, we're going to "go back in time" and look at the beginnings of God's surprising choice for this critical assignment. But let's first begin by calling him Saul, which was the name the apostle Paul was known by before his conversion.

> Paul was one of the most unlikely candidates you could ever imagine to be called by God into the ministry.

RELIGIOUS, BUT MEAN-SPIRITED

Saul was born into a very strict, religious Hebrew environment. In Philippians 3:5, he vividly described the environment into which he was born. He wrote that he was "…an Hebrew of the Hebrews; as touching the law, a Pharisee."

The phrase "an Hebrew of the Hebrews" tells us that Saul was born into an eminently strict Hebrew home. It was a home where the family spoke Hebrew as their primary language and stringently kept all Hebrew religious customs. In every way, Saul was a Hebrew.

Being raised in such a traditional and religious Jewish home also meant that Saul had been taught to disdain the beliefs and behaviors of the Gentile world. In fact, as a child, he was taught to thank God every morning that he was born a Jew and not a Gentile. The darkness of the pagan world was drastically different than all Saul had ever known, and the pagan way of life was considered to be "low life" compared to his familiar world of orthodox Judaism.

Saul was not only religious, but he was also a Pharisee — the strictest of all the religious groups in Israel when it came to adhering to the Law. You might say Saul was at the very top of his "denomination." He was fiercely committed to the religious beliefs and customs of his people, with no tolerance for any form of deviation from his ancestors' faith.

Saul was so full of religious zeal that when Hebrews began to accept Jesus as the Messiah, he was filled with fury against them for deviating from the traditional Jewish faith. Acts 8:3 (*NKJV*) reveals how enraged Saul was with Jewish converts: "As for Saul, he made havoc of the church, entering every house, and dragging off men and women, committing them to prison."

This verse is packed with information about Saul before his conversion. Let's look at it deeper to see how this strong, zealous fervor affected Saul before he came to Christ. You'll see that even though Saul was very "religious," he was an extremely mean-spirited individual. And as is so often the case even today among the ultra-religious, that intolerance drove him to attack and abuse those who held a religious view different than his own.

Acts 8:3 tells us that Saul "made havoc of the church." This phrase "made havoc" comes from a Greek word, which means *to ravage, to ruin, to destroy,* or *to devastate.* This word was used to describe the fate of people who were *mauled to death* by extremely dangerous animals. Often this word depicted the devastation left by wild boars, or wild pigs, that were diseased, vicious, and deadly.

These diseased animals were known not only to *destroy* property and livestock, but also to *maim*, and at times even *kill*, people.

This Greek word translated "made havoc" is the word Luke used in Acts 8:3 to dramatically describe how mean-spirited and ugly Saul's behavior was before he came to Christ. Saul was like an uncontrollable, diseased beast who violently pursued, attacked, and abused people he believed had abandoned their Jewish faith to convert to a new "sect" of those called Christians.

But no one painted a better picture of Paul's grievous manner of life before he came to Christ than the apostle did himself. Let's see what Paul wrote about his old character before he was born again and transformed by the power of God. He actually used horrible words in his first epistle to Timothy to describe his mean-spiritedness before he came to Christ:

> **And I thank Christ Jesus our Lord, who hath enabled me, for that he counted me faithful, putting me into the ministry; who was before a *blasphemer*, and a *persecutor*, and *injurious*....**
>
> **— 1 Timothy 1:12,13**

Paul wrote that he was a *blasphemer*, a *persecutor*, and *injurious*. What do these words mean? What do they tell us about the old Saul — this man who later became the greatest missionary in history and the writer of most of the New Testament after being transformed by the power of Christ?

The word "blasphemer" is from the Greek word *blasphemeo*, which means *to slander; to accuse; to speak against;* or *to speak derogatory words for the purpose of injuring or harming someone's reputation.* It also

> No one painted a better picture of Paul's grievous manner of life before he came to Christ than the apostle did himself.

signifies *profane, foul, unclean language*. However, in general, this word *blasphemeo* refers to *any derogatory speech intended to defame, injure, or harm another's reputation.*

Although Saul had been a very devout Jew, he later used this word "blasphemer" to describe himself in that earlier season of his life. That tells us that although Saul looked outwardly religious, he was internally rotten to the core, and the root of that inner rottenness was revealed by his harsh, mean mouth. It didn't matter that he wore the outer garments of the religious. Saul was spiritually lost, and the angry, bitter stream of words that flowed from his mouth revealed it.

The mouth is the great revealer. It is the outlet, or the "spout," for what is really inside a person.

The hatred raging in Saul's heart manifested visibly in his behavior and could be heard in his words. By using the word "blasphemer" to describe what he was like as an unregenerate man, the apostle was essentially telling us, *"Before Christ, I had a foul mouth."*

> The mouth is the great revealer. It is the outlet, or the "spout," for what is really inside a person.

The word "persecutor" is from the Greek word *dioko*, which means *to hunt, to chase, to persecute,* or *to pursue.* It denoted the actions of a hunter who followed after an animal in order to *apprehend it, capture it,* or *kill it.*

Just as a hunter strategically follows after an animal, Saul mercilessly pursued believers before he came to Christ. Armed with permission from Jewish leaders, he raided homes to search for believers and their meeting places. Like a hunter, Saul was focused on apprehending Christians to imprison them or even deliver them to be murdered, as was the fate of Stephen (*see* Acts 7:58-60).

The third word the apostle Paul used to describe himself before coming to Christ is what the *King James Version* calls "injurious." It is from the Greek word *hubristes*, a word that describes *pleasure derived from inflicting injury on someone.* This may help us understand Saul's "sideline view" as Stephen's killers stoned him to death. It is difficult for us to imagine, but before Saul was converted, he was, by his own admission, so mean-spirited that he derived pleasure from seeing others suffer physical pain. That's a horrible thing to say about someone, but this is precisely what Paul wrote about his own spiritual condition before he was powerfully converted and brought into God's Kingdom.

When one studies all these words Paul used to describe what he was like before coming to Christ when he was still called Saul, the combined meanings serve to underscore why the apostle called himself "the chief of sinners" (*see* 1 Timothy 1:15). Yet amazingly, God initiated reconciliation with Saul and made known to him the divine call He had placed on his life before the foundation of the world (*see* Ephesians 1:4,11; 2:10). The grace of God completely transformed Saul from the inside out. That divine grace instantly released Saul from the guilt of the injustices he had carried out against believers and redirected his life to fulfill God's will. *And this is exactly what God wants to do for you!*

> **The grace of God completely transformed Saul from the inside out. That divine grace instantly released Saul from the guilt of the injustices he had carried out against believers and redirected his life to fulfill God's will.** *And this is exactly what God wants to do for you!*

How Saul's Life Took a New Direction

In approximately 37 AD, Saul and his men made their way toward the city of Damascus. In Saul's possession was official permission from the high priest to hunt for, attack, and imprison followers of Jesus. But along the way, his journey took on a surprising new direction. Something happened on that road that not only completely changed Saul's life — it also affected the course of human history.

Luke wrote about this pivotal event in Acts 9:3-6:

> **And as he** [Saul] **journeyed, he came near Damascus: and suddenly there shined round about him a light from heaven: And he fell to the earth, and heard a voice saying unto him, Saul, Saul, why persecutest thou me?**
>
> **And he said, Who art thou, Lord? And the Lord said, I am Jesus whom thou persecutest: it is hard for thee to kick against the pricks.**
>
> **And he trembling and astonished said, Lord, what wilt thou have me to do? And the Lord said unto him, Arise, and go into the city, and it shall be told thee what thou must do.**

Imagine the scene: Saul was en route to Damascus with murderous hatred in his heart, intent on wreaking more havoc on believers. But the Bible says that as he journeyed, he suddenly saw "…a light from heaven, above the brightness of the sun…." (Acts 26:13). It must have appeared as something like a lightning strike, but it was *the glory of God* — so powerful in its brilliance that it physically knocked Saul to the ground (*see* Acts 9:4).

Then a voice that only Saul could understand spoke to him. To everyone else, the voice was indistinct and unintelligible. In Acts 26:14, Paul related, "…I heard a voice speaking unto me, and saying in the Hebrew tongue, Saul, Saul, why persecutest thou me?…"

Lying on the ground and temporarily incapacitated by the power of God, Saul answered, "…Who art thou, Lord? And he said, I am Jesus whom thou persecutest" (Acts 9:5).

In that moment, the Church's most zealous persecutor called upon the name of the Lord — and Jesus' power reached out to lay hold of him. Saul's life journey instantaneously changed directions as, in a split second, he was saved, delivered, and changed into a champion of truth. Eventually this transformed man launched the first missionary activity in the history of the Church and wrote epistles to various churches, which were so full of Holy Spirit inspiration and revelation that God's people are still being transformed by these divine truths today.

> **Saul's life journey instantaneously changed directions as, in a split second, he was saved, delivered, and changed into a champion of truth.**

GOD DEFINES PAUL'S CALL

The instant Saul was saved, the Holy Spirit entered into his heart, as He does with all newborn believers. And in that same instant, God's plan for Saul's life was literally deposited into his born-again, recreated spirit. All of that took place in that split second Saul called Jesus "Lord" on the road to Damascus (*see* Acts 9:5).

The same thing happened to *you* the moment you gave your life to Christ. In a split second, God's Spirit gave you a new spirit — and in that exact same instant, the will of God was deposited into your spirit and you received His divine plan for your life. You may still not have comprehended God's plan for your life yet, but it's there, deep inside you, and it's very clear and concrete.

Think of it — God's marvelous plan for your life is living and breathing deep inside you right now. Even if your mind hasn't realized or comprehended it all yet, it's there, waiting to be tapped into. And when you finally realize it, embrace it, and begin to pursue it, that divine plan will unleash supernatural power to carry you forward toward its fulfillment.

> **Think of it — God's marvelous plan for your life is living and breathing deep inside you right now.**

Once Saul was saved, the Lord said to him, "...Arise, and go into the city, and it shall be told thee what thou must do" (Acts 9:6). In obedience to this divine instruction, Saul headed toward the city. Because his eyes were still blinded by the radiance of God's glory, Saul couldn't see to walk, so the men accompanying him led him by the hand into Damascus to the house of a man named Judas on Straight Street (see v. 11). Then verse 9 tells us, "And he was three days without sight, and neither did eat nor drink."

We may speculate what Saul went through as this temporary blindness held him stationary during those three days. When a person cannot see, he can only sit — and *think*. And Saul had a lot to think about.

Moments before Saul's conversion, he was a man pursuing with single-eyed focus his mission of arresting, and even giving his approval for the slaughter of, believers. Then Jesus Himself appeared to Saul, and in an instant, he was saved. Afterward, Saul found himself temporarily held captive by blindness that kept him stationary and quiet — thus affording him time to digest everything that had happened to him. For three days, he didn't eat or drink anything, and he could see nothing. He just sat there, thinking about what he had experienced and heard from Christ on that road to Damascus.

To really get the full picture of what Jesus said to Saul on that road, you must read what Saul — who by then was the apostle Paul — related about that event in Acts 26:16,17. As he stood on trial in front of King Agrippa, Paul gave his own testimony of what happened when Jesus appeared to him on the road to Damascus. This was Paul's personal testimony, and he added important personal insights Luke hadn't included in Acts 9:1-9.

These insights explain why Saul had so much to digest in those three days of silence and blindness immediately after his conversion. He told Agrippa what Jesus had told him in that divine encounter:

> **Rise, and stand upon thy feet: for I have appeared unto thee for this purpose, to make thee a minister and a witness both of these things which thou hast seen, and of those things in the which I will appear unto thee; delivering thee from the people, and from *the Gentiles, unto whom now I send thee.***
>
> **— Acts 26:16,17**

Notice Jesus told Saul, "I am sending you to the Gentiles...." This must have been shocking almost beyond belief for Saul to hear that God would send him to the Gentiles. Remember, he was a "Hebrew of the Hebrews" and a Pharisee! He had been raised from childhood to live separately from what Jews considered to be the disgusting, low-life behaviors and customs of Gentiles. *But now God was calling Saul to reach the Gentiles with the Good News of Jesus Christ.*

After hearing these amazing words of divine direction, Saul was held captive for three days, unable to move about freely — unable to do anything except to *think*. For three days, his mind was filled with the words Jesus had said to him. Saul was so shocked at this abrupt change in his life — and the knowledge that Jesus was sending him to the Gentile world — that he couldn't entertain the thought of food or drink. Considering the fact that Saul had been taught from childhood to loathe Gentiles, it is understandable that the very thought of spending the rest of his life with Gentiles took away his desire for food and drink.

What Saul was going through during those three days of temporary blindness is easy for me to understand because of my own personal experience with the call of God. When the Holy Spirit spoke to me and told me to move my family to the USSR, it was not something I had anticipated. It took me totally by surprise. I was willing to do whatever Jesus asked of me. But when I said yes to His call to that part of the world, the very thought of taking that step of faith — and moving my family to such a dangerous part of the world — caused me to become physically ill. I ended up in front of a toilet off and on for nearly 20 hours, vomiting repeatedly as I thought about what this step of obedience would require of my family.

God didn't make me sick; He never makes anyone sick. But in those first days of realizing this new phase of my call, my emotions recoiled at the thought of what He was asking me to do. At that moment, I couldn't even think of food. My whole being was trying to adjust to the call that God had awakened in my heart. Like Saul, it took time for me to fully digest what it meant.

> My whole being was trying to adjust to the call that God had awakened in my heart. Like Saul, it took time for me to fully digest what it meant.

The USSR was not exactly the place I had dreamed about for Denise and me to raise our children. At that moment, our ministry was thriving, and leaving it behind to move to the other side of the world seemed so illogical. I kept thinking, *Lord, do You really want me to move my family into the heart of the USSR, the world's bastion of Communism? Have You forgotten that that's where believers have suffered prison and death for their faith? And You want me to move my wife and sons THERE?"*

Everything in my upbringing as an American said, *"This is an illogical thing to do!"* But God had clearly spoken to me. It was as undeniable as the words Jesus spoke to Saul on the road to Damascus. Yet it was so startling for my mind to come to grips with what Jesus was asking of me that I lived in a stupor for a number of days.

Today as I reflect on those first days of processing what the Lord had instructed me to do, it's difficult for me to fully relate to what I went through, since Russia has been our beloved home for so many years. But during those early hours and days of adjusting to God's plan, I'd sit frozen and paralyzed, stunned at what He had revealed to me about our assignment. Like Saul, I couldn't eat or drink for days.

God Confirms What He Tells You To Do!

In Saul's vision on the road to Damascus, Jesus instructed him to go to Damascus, where he would receive further direction (*see* Acts 9:8-12). Although this supernatural event was so spectacular, Saul could have wondered later, *Am I losing my mind? Did Jesus Christ really appear to me? Did I just call Him the Lord of my life? What kind of life-altering course change have I just made?*

Surely these or similar thoughts would have passed through Saul's mind, as they would yours if you were in his place. Did Jesus really appear to him in blazing glory, changing his life course and telling him go into Damascus (as a blind man, no less) to seek further direction?

The men leading Saul into Damascus eventually took Saul to Judas's house on Straight Street. Regardless of how it happened that Saul ended up at Judas' house, each step Saul took in obedience to that heavenly vision served as a confirmation that what he had seen and heard was genuine.

You see, the call on Saul's life created such a radical change of direction that he *needed* confirmation to know he was headed in the right direction. As a strict Jew who had been highly educated in the Law, Saul never would have imagined — not in his wildest dreams — that God would ever ask him to go to the Gentile world. It was such a radical, dramatic change of direction that Saul needed confirmation along the way to help him know he was really hearing from the Lord.

That's exactly what happened to me when God called my family to the Soviet Union. When God told me what He wanted our family to do, His direction represented a *very* radical change of direction for our lives. Although I was willing to do whatever He asked, I really needed confirmation to know I wasn't dreaming it up or making a big mistake.

> **I'm so grateful that God loves us so much that He provides confirmation along the way to let us know we are on track. He knows when we need it.**

I'm so grateful that God loves us so much that He provides confirmation along the way to let us know we are on track. He knows when we need it.

Regarding this call to move to the USSR, Denise and I received *many* confirmations that I had heard God correctly, and some of these confirmations happened over and over again. They may not have meant much to anyone else, but to us, it was as if God was shouting in our ears: *"You are on track!"*

Denise and I knew that God could require blind obedience, and we were willing to blindly obey. But we were so thankful for every confirmation that God provided along the way to reassure us that we were on course with His plan and that we weren't making a mistake.

If you're determined to follow God's will for your life, you will also face your own "crossroad moments" when Jesus gives you a new assignment that requires more of you than you have to give in the natural. As you prepare to step forward by faith to take on the new challenge, it's vital that you keep your eyes and ears open to see and hear the Lord's confirmations when He provides them.

As Saul sat in that house in Damascus, pondering all that had happened to him, he had a second vision. In this vision, he saw a man named Ananias coming to pray for his sight to be restored. And Acts 9 tells us that at precisely the same time Saul had his second vision, a disciple named Ananias also had a vision in which Jesus gave him specific instructions, saying: "...Arise, and go into the street which is called Straight, and enquire in the house of Judas for one called Saul, of Tarsus: for, behold, he prayeth, and hath seen in a vision a man named Ananias coming in, and putting his hand on him, that he might receive his sight" (vv. 11,12).

Ananias was well aware of Saul's notorious reputation for persecuting believers, for Saul's malevolent actions were very well known among the Christians of the region. Even the news of Saul's plans to come to Damascus to persecute believers had already reached the ears of the Christians who lived in that city. So when Ananias heard Jesus' instructions to go pray for Saul, he voiced his fears to the Lord: "...Lord, I have heard by many of this man, how much evil he hath done to thy saints at Jerusalem: And here he hath authority from the chief priests to bind all that call on thy name" (Acts 9:13,14).

But Jesus said to him, "…Go thy way: for he is a chosen vessel unto me, to bear my name before the Gentiles, and kings, and the children of Israel: For I will shew him how great things he must suffer for my name's sake" (vv. 15,16).

Saul wasn't the only one who needed confirmation! Put yourself in Ananias's shoes. In that situation, you would probably need confirmation as well before you paid a visit to Saul of Tarsus! *Remember, this was a killer of Christians.* Just imagine the thoughts that would have raced through your mind as you got ready to head toward your meeting with this notorious, mean-spirited man who had originally come to town to kill people like you.

If Ananias hadn't known beforehand, he discovered as he traveled to obey the Lord's directive that there really *was* a street called Straight. That would have certainly served as a confirmation to his heart that the instruction he had received was truly from the Lord. And when Ananias inquired to know if a house existed on that street belonging to a man named Judas — and he discovered that there *was* — that had to be another giant confirmation for him. With these multiple confirmations fortifying his resolve to obey the Lord, Ananias boldly knocked on the door to find Saul and do what Jesus had asked him to do.

Acts 9:17 says that Ananias "…went his way, and entered into the house; and putting his hands on him said, Brother Saul, the Lord, even Jesus, that appeared unto thee in the way as thou camest, hath sent me, that thou mightest receive thy sight, and be filled with the Holy Ghost." Verse 18 continues, "And immediately there fell from his eyes as it had been scales: and he received sight forthwith, and arose, and was baptized."

So we see that the account of this amazing encounter is *filled* with multiple confirmations!

- First, Saul had a spectacular vision of Jesus that completely changed his life course in an instant and temporarily blinded him.

- Saul had a second vision in which he saw a man named Ananias coming to pray for him.

- Ananias had a vision that told him to go to a street called Straight.

- In this vision, Ananias heard that a house was on that street belonging to a man named Judas.

- Ananias was told to go to that house and lay hands on Saul of Tarsus — *and* that Saul would receive his restored sight.

Both men — Saul and Ananias — needed confirmation to know they weren't hallucinating or imagining what they had respectively seen and heard. Every step along the way, each confirmation provided the assurance that they had really heard from God and the encouragement to keep going forward.

When Ananias saw Saul, Ananias knew he was on track, and it gave him confidence to step forward to pray for Saul and prophesy to him. And when Saul heard that a man had come to the door whose name was Ananias, he knew this was a man whom God had sent, and it opened his heart to receive whatever Ananias had to say to him. Both men were prepared and empowered by various confirmations along the way that they recognized as coming from the Lord.

> Every step along the way, each confirmation provided the assurance that they had really heard from God and the encouragement to keep going forward.

'GENTILES, KINGS, AND THE CHILDREN OF ISRAEL'

When Ananias prayed for Saul, he delivered the prophetic word that God had given him concerning Saul's life. Jesus had told Ananias that Saul was "…a chosen vessel unto me, to bear my name before the *Gentiles*, and *kings*, and the *children of Israel*" (Acts 9:15).

But wait — this was *not* the first time Saul had heard this word of divine direction! Do you remember when he was in front of King Agrippa and he testified of what Jesus had said to him on the road to Damascus? Jesus had told Saul, "…Rise, and stand upon thy feet: for I have appeared unto thee for this purpose, to make thee a minister and a witness both of these things which thou hast seen, and of those things in the which I will appear unto thee; delivering thee from the people, and from *the Gentiles, unto whom now I send thee*"(Acts 26:16,17).

So when Saul heard these prophetic words spoken from the mouth of Ananias, what he heard was another confirmation. If it had been the first time he had heard those words, he could have argued that Ananias was wrong or misled. But Jesus had already explicitly told Saul while Saul was still on the road to Damascus that He was sending him to the Gentile world. Ananias' prophetic words were, in fact, a reaffirmation of what Christ had already said to Saul.

A complete stranger repeated exactly what Jesus had privately told Saul three days earlier! The odds of that happening by chance are almost scientifically impossible. So when Saul heard these words, it served as another confirmation from the heart of God to reassure him that he had truly heard from Him regarding His profound will and plan for his life.

Through Saul's own experience with Christ on the road to Damascus, and then by the confirming words later spoken by Ananias, God affirmed to Saul the three-pronged call He had ordained for his life. It is the belief of some, including me, that this was the divine priority that God set in place for Paul's ministry. We will proceed in this book with the foundational premise that:

- First and foremost, Saul was called to take the Gospel to the Gentiles.

- Second, he was to represent Jesus to governmental authorities and kings.

- Third and last of all, he was to bear witness of Jesus the Messiah to the children of Israel.

This was the prophetic order of God's will for Saul's life. But here's the profound truth I want you to see:

God's plan for EVERY PERSON'S life is imparted to his spirit the moment he is born again!

When the Holy Spirit comes into the human heart at the moment of salvation, He brings God's plan for that individual with Him. It may take time for a believer's mind to catch up with his heart's knowledge of that divine plan, but his heart knows nonetheless.

Since this is true, it means the will of God for *your* life has been in you since the moment you surrendered to Christ. You may not have grasped it yet, but that marvelous divine plan is lying inside you — waiting to explode into your mind so you can lay hold of it and begin to walk it out.

> **The will of God for *your* life has been in you since the moment you surrendered to Christ — waiting to explode into your mind so you can lay hold of it and begin to walk it out.**

FOR WHAT PURPOSE DID JESUS
SEND PAUL TO THE GENTILES?

In Acts 26:18, the apostle Paul quoted to King Agrippa the words that Jesus had spoken to his heart at the moment of his conversion. Jesus had told Saul that He was sending him to the Gentiles "to open their eyes, and to turn them from darkness to light, and from the power of Satan unto God, that they may receive forgiveness of sins, and inheritance among them which are sanctified by faith that is in me."

In this verse, Jesus outlined five specific things Paul was to accomplish *among the Gentiles*. He was to:

1. Open their eyes to truth.

2. Turn them from darkness to light.

3. Turn them from the power of Satan to God's power.

4. Teach them to receive forgiveness of sin.

5. Show them how to activate their inheritance through faith in Jesus.

Although God's call on Paul's life was three-pronged in its reach, it was first and foremost *to the Gentiles*. Paul confirmed this specialized life assignment numerous times throughout his epistles (*see* Romans 1:5,13,14; Galatians 1:16; 2:7,8), recognizing his unique call and apostleship to the Gentiles. As you read on in the following chapters, you'll see why this point is so important for you to understand.

For Saul to be sent to the Gentiles was such a radical idea for him to digest. Although he had heard these instructions from the mouth of Jesus Himself, Saul undoubtedly mulled them over in his mind during those three days in that Damascus house as he sat without sight. *I'm a Jew*, he may have thought. *How could God send me to the Gentiles?*

Whatever Saul's thoughts were in the days following his life-altering encounter with Jesus on the road to Damascus, God knew that he needed confirmation, so He sent Ananias. And when Saul received that prophetic word through this obedient emissary of the Lord, it was exactly what Saul needed in order to be assured beyond any doubt that he had heard from God.

PROPHETIC WORDS CONFIRM
WHAT GOD HAS ALREADY SAID

True prophecy almost always confirms what God has already spoken to your own heart. This is precisely what you find in the case of Saul and Ananias in Acts chapter 9.

Over the years, there have been numerous people who have come to me with what they thought were "words from the Lord" that they needed to give me. Often these "words" didn't fit with a single thing the Holy Spirit had ever spoken to my heart. Of course, I always want to be respectful and open to the fact that God could use someone to say something new to me. But when the word given is far afield from what I know He has already said to me, I'm usually confident that I don't need to take it seriously. On the other hand, if it affirms something that God's Spirit has already been speaking to me, I listen very carefully.

When the Lord speaks to my heart, I know His voice (*see* John 10:27). I have been greatly encouraged in instances when someone has repeated to me something the Holy Spirit had already spoken to my heart. Those moments are *powerful*. They are confirming words regarding very specific direction Jesus has given me, and they provide the support and encouragement I need to move forward in obedience to His instructions.

A genuine prophetic word regarding God's will for your life will confirm what He has already told you, and it will empower you to face the future with confidence.

If God is going to speak something significant to you about His will for your life, it is likely that He will tell you personally about it first. For instance, He may speak to you during prayer or reveal to you as you study the Bible that a change is coming. Or perhaps you and your spouse are praying together, and suddenly you both begin to sense an upcoming change. Or you may receive that same word of direction while sitting in church and listening to your pastor preach. Later the Lord brings someone to you who says to you, "I sense a change is coming to your life." That kind of confirming word — affirming what you already know — is *powerful.*

> A genuine prophetic word regarding God's will for your life will confirm what He has already told you, and it will empower you to face the future with confidence.

That's what happened to Saul — and that's what happened to Ananias. They both heard from Jesus, and then the steps they each took along the way *confirmed* that they had indeed heard from Him.

If you need a confirming word concerning the will of God for your life, the Holy Spirit will be faithful to orchestrate it. And the bigger and more "out of the ordinary" your assignment seems to be — the more dramatic the confirmation will likely be. Whatever the case regarding the call God has ordained you to fulfill, He knows exactly what you need to hear. He wants you fully assured that you are on track and running the race He has set before you!

THINK ABOUT IT

1. Describe some of the experiences in your past that have revealed the unique "fingerprints" of God's call on your life — things that can only be explained by the touch of *His* hand and His great desire for you to walk on His prearranged path for you every day of your life.

2. What has God revealed to you about His plan for your life? Write down any specific details He has spoken to you and how He has confirmed them over time. Don't forget those confirmations. Write them down!

3. Up to the moment Jesus called Saul, Saul was adamantly opposed to Him. But the Holy Spirit radically changed Saul's heart and made him one of the greatest advocates of His Kingdom who has ever lived. What radical changes has God made in *you* that demonstrate clear evidence of His life-changing power?

CHAPTER TWO

PLACED IN THE RIGHT ENVIRONMENT FOR YOUR GIFTS TO DEVELOP

When God calls you, His intent is to fully equip and prepare you to effectively complete your assignment. He will use every aspect of who you are and where you came from to bring about His will in your life. He uses your background, your level of education, your past occupations, and everything else you've accumulated from your life experiences. Many times He will also lead you into new territory where you are surrounded by unfamiliar faces in order to teach you lessons that you couldn't learn any other way.

AN UNEXPECTED OPPORTUNITY

I grew up in the city of Tulsa, so I always thought I would attend Oral Roberts University (ORU), which continues to be one of the premier Christian universities in the world. ORU happened to be located in my hometown, so I was fervent about attending that particular university after I graduated from high school. In fact, I even began taking a class there while I was still in high school in order to try to get a jump-start on my education.

Every week I attended a class taught by Oral Roberts himself, sitting on the front row, and hanging on to every word he said.

Finally, the time came for me to graduate from high school, and I eagerly anticipated attending ORU full-time that fall. However, one day as I was praying about my future, the Holy Spirit spoke to my heart very clearly and actually *forbade* me to attend ORU. I was completely stunned!

"Why don't You want me to go to ORU, Lord?" I asked incredulously. "There's no better place for a young man like me than Oral Roberts University!"

The Holy Spirit answered me: *"Because there are things I want to teach you that you can only learn somewhere else. You'd be in a good environment at ORU, but you would miss the greater things I want to impart to you that are important for your future."*

I really wanted to attend ORU, but I knew I needed to follow the Holy Spirit's leading. So I made the choice to forego Oral Roberts University and to enroll at a secular university in our state that He led me to instead. As that first school year progressed, the reason for attending that university became apparent as doors of ministry opened to me that might otherwise have been left shut if I had attended a Christian university.

It was in this secular-university environment where I first began to get deeply involved in the ministry. My earliest experience in teaching the Bible took place in the university church, and because unbelievers constantly surrounded me, I learned how to communicate Christ to nonbelievers. These experiences familiarized me with the academic community's objections to the Gospel, which in turn sharpened my ability to be an effective witness for the Lord.

That university is also where I began to study Greek in earnest. These studies allowed me to delve deeper into the Word of God by analyzing the New Testament in its original Greek. Before long, believers at the university church I attended began to approach me if they had a question about the Greek New Testament.

Through these interactions, I saw how I could fill a vital niche in the Body of Christ by utilizing my understanding of New Testament Greek to open up Scripture in such a way that listeners could gain new insight about the Word of God. The skills I gleaned from this discipline profoundly affected my entire life. My approach to studying was completely reshaped, laying the foundations for my teaching ministry that would touch the lives of many thousands of people across the world in the years to come.

THE RIGHT PLACE AT THE RIGHT TIME

When I look back on my years at that secular university, I can clearly see why it was God's plan for me to attend that secular school. It was a necessary training ground that provided me with the foundational skills I needed to succeed in ministry, and I am very thankful for that experience.

As wonderful as Oral Roberts University is, it was not the right place for me. God wanted me at a secular university so He could impart both natural and spiritual equipment to me that I would not have received in another environment. And to top it off, I met Denise at the university church! That connection was a *crucial* part of God's plan for me and another big reason He led me to attend that particular university.

Your environment — *the surroundings and conditions in which you live and operate* — is important! Being in the right place at the right time according to God's plan for your life is critical to fulfilling His will for your life. God will use specific people and places — and the opportunities that arise in the environment of those right places — to shape you, sharpen your gifts, and prepare you to do His will.

> Being in the right place at the right time according to God's plan for your life is critical to fulfilling His will for your life.

Are you where God has directed you to be? It might be that the place to which you are called is outside your comfort zone, and you wish you could escape to somewhere else far away. However, if you know in your heart that God has spoken a word over your life, don't second-guess Him — *trust* Him. Trust that He is working to fully develop the gifts He has placed within you so you can fulfill your divine mandate. *He knows exactly what you need!*

MY SPECIAL PLACE TO GROW

When I think of being in the right environment at the right time, my mind immediately goes to that university church I attended during my college years. As I mentioned earlier, it was where I met my future wife Denise and where I began to take my very first steps toward building a public teaching ministry.

I'll never forget the first time I attended a service at that church. I was so excited to be a part of a congregation filled with young people who were excited about the things of God. And what a group it was! Many of the young men and women who called that church their spiritual home came from "colorful" backgrounds, to say the least. In fact, quite a few were former hippies who used to smoke marijuana and support a myriad of radical political causes. Having grown up in a denominational church surrounded by denominational Christians, I was definitely *not* in the church environment I was accustomed to!

One thing I really loved about that group of young believers was their openness to and their fervency for the work of the Holy Spirit. They were *on fire* for the Lord! Very few of them had grown up in church or had any sort of religious background whatsoever. They had come to college to party, smoke dope, and join any radical cause they could find. But then unexpectedly someone shared the Gospel with them, and they received Jesus Christ into their hearts.

When these young people came to Jesus, they brought the same passion to the things of God that they had previously directed toward the world. They earnestly wanted to evangelize, preach, pray, prophesy, and experience spiritual dreams and visions from the Lord. When I walked into the church building, I witnessed a congregation exploding with life. When it was time to prophesy, people would often line up to give their words from God. It was the most exciting environment I had ever been in!

In addition to the young people who had little or no religious upbringing, God had also strategically placed a few people in the group who had a solid foundation in the Word of God — including me. The denominational church I had grown up in placed a strong emphasis on sound doctrine, and because of that, I had been taught the Bible all my life.

My father and mother imparted the Scriptures to me when I was still a young child, and our pastor was a profound Bible teacher who taught the principles of the Word in a balanced, thorough manner. Even though the denominational church I grew up in didn't allow the gifts of the Holy Spirit to operate, overall I was given a solid, scriptural foundation upon which to build my life and ministry. I am so thankful for this spiritual upbringing!

So there were the free-spirited new believers in our university church — sitting right next to a number of folks like me who had a strong background in the Bible. Having more seasoned believers alongside the enthusiastic new believers and those who fervently pursued spiritual manifestations made for a powerful mix in our congregation. In that environment, my Bible education and study of classical Greek proved to be an important ingredient in our young college church. I learned how to move freely with the Holy Spirit and to blend that supernatural work with a solid, intelligent exposition of the Bible.

> My Bible education and study of classical Greek proved to be an important ingredient in our young college church. I learned how to move freely with the Holy Spirit and to blend that supernatural work with a solid, intelligent exposition of the Bible.

Those among us who were well versed in the Word of God were able to discern what was doctrinally sound and what was contrary to the teaching of Scripture. This became extremely important as the church began to move into new realms of the Spirit. God had created the right balance to keep the church healthy and moving forward.

THE CHURCH AT ANTIOCH

Paul played a *major* role in the founding of the Early Church. God used him to write almost two-thirds of the New Testament, and his epistles have guided the Body of Christ for nearly 2,000 years. However, Paul — then Saul — had to go somewhere entirely unexpected early in his Christian life in order to come to an accurate understanding of God's vision of the Church.

Soon after Saul's life-changing conversion on the road to Damascus, he traveled to Jerusalem, eager to connect with the disciples there and begin his ministry. Given Saul's background as a former rabbi who spoke fluent Hebrew, it's easy to understand why Jerusalem would be the natural choice on which to focus his efforts. After all, he was so intimately acquainted with the Jewish culture, tradition, and religious thought that permeated that city. However, God had called Saul first and foremost to bring the Gospel to the Gentile world. And although God did use key parts of Saul's past to equip him for his call, Jerusalem's predominantly Jewish environment could not adequately prepare him to fulfill this ministry.

> God had called Saul first and foremost to bring the Gospel to the Gentile world. And although God did use key parts of Saul's past to equip him for his call, Jerusalem's predominantly Jewish environment could not adequately prepare him for this ministry.

Saul's stay in Jerusalem didn't last long. The Gospel message he boldly proclaimed in the synagogues soon after his arrival enraged the local Jewish leadership, and they conspired to kill him. When the local believers learned of this plot against Saul's life, they helped him covertly leave the city and then sent him off to his hometown of Tarsus. There Saul remained until God was ready to usher him into the next phase of his calling, during which the sure foundations of his ministry would be laid and his Christian walk would be strengthened and advanced by leaps and bounds.

The proving ground for Saul would be the city of Antioch, a city located approximately 250 miles north of Jerusalem in modern-day Turkey. It was also in Antioch where he would later begin to be called Paul.

Antioch was the third largest city in the Roman Empire during New Testament times; only Rome and Alexandria exceeded it in size. Situated on a crossroads between East and West, it was a thriving commercial center and a true melting pot of cultures and peoples. The city's population was also composed primarily of Gentiles, which was a very important factor for Saul, given the nature of his calling.

The multiplicity of cultures found within the thriving urban environment of Antioch had produced a colorful and diverse Christian community. The Gospel was first brought to Antioch in the wake of Stephen's martyrdom, and many who resided there warmly received the message. In fact, this city experienced a revival as pagans and Jews alike left behind their old lives and accepted Jesus as their Lord and Savior. Before long, a thriving church had been established in Antioch, and the believers began to actively evangelize their city and the surrounding region. During his time with this congregation, Saul regularly ministered alongside Gentiles and learned to communicate effectively with them. These experiences would do much to equip him for the epic apostolic journeys that he would later embark upon across the Roman Empire.

From the outset of the Antioch church, the work grew rapidly until it was second in size only to the church of Jerusalem. However, despite the distinction of these churches as having the two largest congregations during the mid-First Century, they were very different in nature. Many of the believers in Antioch were Gentiles who came from pagan backgrounds, whereas the believers in Jerusalem were nearly all of Jewish ancestry. As we will see, this disparity resulted in two different approaches to the Christian walk.

WHY NOT JERUSALEM?

Antioch's rich, diverse environment was God's "right place" for Saul in that season so he could become equipped and fully prepared for ministry. A brand-new move of the Spirit was taking place in that city — and, by following God's calling to move there, Saul put himself in a position to receive a completely fresh perspective of the Body of Christ. During his time in Antioch, he learned important lessons from what he saw and experienced that he could never have learned if he had stayed in Jerusalem.

> A brand-new move of the Spirit was taking place in that city — and, by following God's calling to move there, Saul put himself in a position to receive a completely fresh perspective of the Body of Christ.

The book of Acts records that in the earliest years of the Church, the Holy Spirit's activity was focused in the city of Jerusalem. Jerusalem was where the Holy Spirit was first poured out on the Day of Pentecost. It was where Peter preached his first great sermon that resulted in the conversion of thousands of unsaved people. And it was in Jerusalem that the apostles worked powerful miracles throughout the city.

The new wine of the Holy Spirit had been poured out first in Jerusalem — but as the years passed, a significant problem arose. By the time of Saul's conversion, the church of Jerusalem had become in many respects *an old, inflexible wineskin.*

In Mark 2:22 (*NKJV*), Jesus said, "And no one puts new wine into old wineskins; or else the new wine bursts the wineskins, the wine is spilled, and the wineskins are ruined. But new wine must be put into new wineskins." This analogy actually appears in three of the four gospels (*see* Matthew 9:17; Mark 2:22; and Luke

5:37-39), and it teaches the importance of being ever-receptive to the working of the Spirit.

During the time of the New Testament, wineskins were watertight containers, usually crafted from pliable goatskin, that were used to hold wine as it aged. When new wine was put in a wineskin, it would continue to ferment. This fermentation would produce gas as a byproduct, which would cause the wineskin to expand and stretch. However, if new wine was poured into an old wineskin that had already been stretched on multiple occasions until it was no longer flexible, the subsequent expansion of the gas could cause the material to burst, spilling the wine and destroying the bag.

Just like an "old wineskin," the church of Jerusalem had grown inflexible. As a result, God's expanding purposes for the Church — to extend the message of the Gospel into the Gentile world and to the ends of the earth — could no longer be contained within just the city of Jerusalem.

There were two key reasons for this transformation. The first was that the believers in Jerusalem were preoccupied with tradition and rules. Jerusalem had been the center of Judaism for many centuries. Consequently, the city epitomized the rituals, ceremonies, rules, and regulations of the Jewish religion. Because the congregation in Jerusalem was primarily comprised of people who had been devout Jews before their conversion, many carried these Jewish customs over into their Christian walk. The religious traditions of these believers' past eventually became entrenched in the new church, and as a result, the congregation wasn't flexible enough to willingly move with God as He sought to advance His Church.

When the new wine of the Spirit was poured out in their midst, the church of Jerusalem tried to rigidly contain it within the context of Judaism. For example, even from its infancy, the congregation in Jerusalem squabbled over the issue of circumcision. Fierce arguments ensued as various factions within the church debated how much of the Law should be kept. This argument and others like it caused schisms to form within the church, preventing the Holy Spirit from continuing to move as mightily as He had in the beginning.

The second reason the church of Jerusalem had become like an old wineskin was that the believers initially believed that the Gospel was for the Jews only and that Gentiles could not receive salvation. This misguided and very narrow mindset severely limited their point of view on many vital doctrinal questions during the early years of the Church's existence — and as a result, the work of the Holy Spirit among them became significantly restricted.

> The religious traditions of these believers' past eventually became entrenched in the new church, and as a result, the congregation wasn't flexible enough to willingly move with God as He sought to advance His Church.

ONE IN CHRIST

The exclusion of Gentiles from the church at Jerusalem also had the negative consequence of eliminating diversity from their congregation. Only one nationality was represented within the church — former Jews who were still very Judaic in their views. This was not a true picture of the new man God was creating. It was not — *and will never be* — His will for the makeup of any congregation to be restricted to one particular race, nationality, or ethnicity. The Bible says:

And this is God's plan: Both Gentiles and Jews who believe the Good News share equally in the riches inherited

by God's children. Both are part of the same body, and both enjoy the promise of blessings because they belong to Christ Jesus.

— Ephesians 3:6 *NLT*

The Body of Christ is intended to be a mixture of people from all nations. If we attempt to restrict the membership of our churches to a single race or nationality, we will derail our mission. When we receive salvation, all considerations of color and nationality disappear because such distinctions do not exist in the mind of Christ.

When Jesus looks at His Church, He doesn't see rich or poor, Jew or Gentile, circumcised or uncircumcised, male or female — He simply sees one unified family. We are all one in Christ (*see* Galatians 3:28; Colossians 3:11). What a phenomenal revelation this is!

> If we attempt to restrict the membership of our churches to a single race or nationality, we will derail our mission. When we receive salvation, all considerations of color and nationality disappear because such distinctions do not exist in the mind of Christ.

However, Saul probably could never have never received this special revelation of the Church if he had stayed in Jerusalem. The congregation in Jerusalem was very proud of their Jewish roots, and their wrong beliefs prevented them from readily acknowledging that God could work through people of all types and backgrounds. Saul was called to minister to the Gentile world first and foremost. If he had based his ministry in Jerusalem — which, as we've seen, was primarily a Jewish church filled with Jewish people and Jewish thinking — he likely would have been unprepared to minister to the Gentiles.

Consequently, God orchestrated events that led Saul to the church of Antioch, where a diverse congregation provided him with an environment in which he could learn how to minister to the Gentile world. There in Antioch, Saul was able to see firsthand the grace of God working through people of many different nationalities, ethnicities, and social classes. This experience engrained in him a multiracial mindset that allowed him to see believers of every background just as Jesus does: *All* are equal partners in the Body of Christ.

Saul's story demonstrates the importance of following the leading of the Holy Spirit and being in the right place at the right time. Antioch was a proving ground for Saul where he received ministerial training that he could never have received in the Jewish congregation of Jerusalem. This was instrumental in furthering Saul's spiritual development and transforming him into the mighty man of God he grew to be.

How about you?

- Is the place where you live and serve adequately equipping and preparing you to fulfill God's calling for your life? You may not always, in every season, be able to readily ascertain this fact at first. But you can trust God to keep you on track — at the right place at the right time — while you maintain an attitude of commitment and consecration to His larger plan.

- What kind of vital life lessons is God teaching you through the circumstances and situations in which you find yourself?

These are important questions to ask yourself. If you're not in the right place — the place God has ordained for you to be — it will hinder you from becoming fully prepared for whatever lies ahead in His plan for your life. At worst, it could completely prevent you from fulfilling God's plan if adjustments or course corrections aren't made when He attempts to move you from one place to another in life.

If you are in the right place, you can be sure that the people around you and the circumstances you face will help prepare and equip you for the days ahead. Still, you must make sure you remain a pliable new wineskin, even when you are in your place of purpose. In other words, it's important to continually keep your eyes, ears, and heart open to recognize and embrace the way God's Spirit is moving in each season to the furtherance of His greater plan and purposes.

ANTIOCH — A NEW WINESKIN

After Acts chapter 8, the church of Jerusalem is rarely mentioned in Scripture. Although the city of Jerusalem had always been dear to the heart of God, it appears that the primary work of the Spirit shifted from Jerusalem to Antioch soon after Saul's arrival. It was Antioch, not Jerusalem, that became Saul's home base throughout all of his early missionary journeys.

> The church of Antioch was a new wineskin. The believers in that city were flexible and open to a fresh move of the Holy Spirit, and their faith was not fettered by the religious traditions of their past.

The church of Antioch was a new wineskin; it was like a clean slate or a chalkboard that had never been written on. The believers in that city were flexible and open to a fresh move of the Holy Spirit, and their faith was not fettered by the religious traditions of their past. They didn't have any religious hang-ups, and the majority of the congregation knew very little, if anything, about the Jewish customs, rites, and ceremonies that preoccupied many of the Jewish believers in Jerusalem. Thus, the believers of Antioch were free to receive new revelation from God without being weighed down or distracted by their religious upbringing.

God placed Saul into this ripe environment for a reason. By being constantly surrounded by fervent, open-minded believers during a crucial stage of his spiritual development, Saul learned how to flow freely with the Holy Spirit. If he had remained in Jerusalem, his growth would have been stifled by the narrow-minded, religious vision of the Church that had taken root in that city. In Jerusalem, he could not have openly taught the type of new revelations he received in Antioch because many of the believers in Jerusalem would have dismissed them outright as being too radical. However, in Antioch, Saul was free to develop his teaching gift in a supportive, non-threatening environment.

Antioch became a spiritual training ground for Saul and countless other believers during the First Century. When God moved the hub of His Spirit's activity to that city, He imparted His new vision to the believers there. It was in that environment that God was able to impart to Saul the revelation of what the Church of Jesus Christ was actually supposed to look like.

What would have happened if Saul had ignored the Holy Spirit's prompting and stayed in Jerusalem? As a former rabbi and Pharisee who spoke fluent Hebrew, Saul would have easily gravitated toward a Judaic view of Christianity. He could have missed out completely on God's revelation of the Church, and his spiritual development and ability to connect with the Gentile world would have been greatly hindered.

> **What would have happened if Saul had ignored the Holy Spirit's prompting and stayed in Jerusalem?**

DIVERSE SPIRITUAL LEADERSHIP

One of the main factors that made the church of Antioch such a great environment was the diversity of its spiritual leadership. With the addition of Saul and his ministry partner, Barnabas, there was a healthy range of ages among those in positions of authority. This is significant, because younger and older leaders all bring something unique to the table. For a ministry to function effectively, it is important to have both present. Young leaders are often more open to new ideas and are flexible concerning a fresh move of God's Spirit. As such, they bring a much-needed vitality to the Body of Christ. On the other hand, older leaders often bring rock-solid stability, experience, and a firmer understanding of the Word of God.

Balance is very important when it comes to spiritual leadership. If there are too many young leaders in a church, that congregation can become imbalanced, unstable, and immature. On the other hand, too many older leaders can cause a church to become limited by a strict adherence to tradition and an unwillingness to change or try new things. However, having the right mix of young and old leaders will bring life, vitality, and stability to a church, making it feel as fresh and exciting as it is well-balanced and doctrinally sound. The church of Antioch was just such a diverse mixture of social class, education, and age.

To understand just how unique the environment at Antioch actually was, let's look for a moment at what the Bible says about their spiritual leadership. Acts 13:1 records:

> **Now there were in the church that was at Antioch certain prophets and teachers; as Barnabas, and Simeon that was called Niger, and Lucius of Cyrene, and Manaen, which had been brought up with Herod the tetrarch, and Saul.**

Five leaders are mentioned in this verse — Saul, Barnabas, Simeon, Lucius, and Manaen. Of these men of God, two had a Hebrew background (Saul and Barnabas), and the other three (Simeon, Lucius, and Manaen) were Gentiles. This was a break from past tradition. For the first time, Jews and Gentiles were serving the Lord together as equal partners in the Body of Christ.

Although the information provided about these men in Acts 13:1 is limited, some knowledge about their lives can be gleaned. For example:

- *Barnabas* was a Levite from the Gentile country of Cyprus, which was a region in Greece (*see* Acts 4:36). He was a distant Jew descended from the tribe of Levi. Because he was raised so far from Jerusalem, it is likely that he didn't grow up around the strict religious environment that was so characteristic of that city.

- *Simeon* is referred to in Scripture as "Niger," which is the Latin word meaning *black*. Scholars speculate that this indicates Simeon was probably a black man from Africa and may have even been the slave of a Roman family. Regardless, he served in a position of authority in the church of Antioch.

- *Lucius of Cyrene* was from the region of Cyrene in northern Africa. Some speculate that this may actually have been Luke. Others argue that Lucius was a man of North African heritage. The name "Lucius" actually means *light* or *bright*. Regardless of the identity of this man, it seems he had come to Antioch from Northern Africa.

- *Manaen* is recorded to have been brought up with Herod the tetrarch and was, in fact, probably a relative of the family of Herod. Because Manaen was Roman and likely descended from the royal family, he had received a Roman education. This is especially significant because educated Romans were raised to look down on foreigners as being uncouth barbarians who were classed as "less" than Romans. Manaen's position, alongside other ethnicities and skin colors, lets us know that he had broken free from the prejudices of his upbringing to work alongside two Africans and two Jews who were brothers in the Lord.

- The last leader in the group was the apostle Paul, who was still called Saul at the time of this supernatural gathering in the church of Antioch. Saul was born into a very well-connected, tremendously wealthy Jewish family who were also Roman citizens. Being raised in a wealthy home, Saul was afforded the best education that money could buy. He had also been theologically trained for his former positions as a rabbi and Pharisee. Consequently, Saul was the most religiously instructed and possessed the greatest breadth of scriptural knowledge of any of his peers among the Antioch church leadership.

To assemble this particular group in the First Century broke all norms of society and was truly a supernatural situation that only God could arrange. By directing Saul to Antioch, the Holy Spirit placed him in a multiracial environment where he could learn to serve side by side with Gentiles and Jews alike.

WHAT PAUL BROUGHT TO THE TABLE

Saul provided the congregation of Antioch with a solid foundation of the Word of God — a dynamic I also experienced when I brought my years of Bible training and study of classical Greek to the university church I served at during my time in college. Saul's years of study and Jewish heritage provided him with a wealth of knowledge. Having him on their teaching staff gave the believers in Antioch unprecedented access to an expert on Jewish culture and the Old Testament. Whether the subject was the story of creation, the Old Testament covenants, praise and worship,

Jesus' lineage, Messianic prophecies, the Shekinah glory of God, or simply Jewish history — all of it was comfortable territory for Saul. As a trained rabbi and theologian, he was like a fish in water when it came to these significant topics. They represented his former identity and were his field of expertise.

It is not difficult to imagine how expounding on the Old Testament in a thorough and balanced manner would have quickly become Saul's niche within the church of Antioch. His fellow believers undoubtedly treasured his knowledge and wisdom. In a sense, Saul served as the congregation's walking Hebrew concordance and Bible commentary! And because he was well versed in the Word of God, Saul was also able to discern what was doctrinally sound and what was contrary to the teaching of Scripture.

This became extremely important as the church of Antioch began to move into realms of the Spirit that were new to them and to receive new revelation they had never heard before. Saul brought just the right balance to the environment to keep the church securely founded while growing in its spiritual capacity.

WHAT PAUL GAINED
IN THE ENVIRONMENT OF ANTIOCH

As I said at the beginning of this chapter, God will use your environment — the people, places, and opportunities around you — to shape and sharpen your gifts. And while He is in the process of developing your gifts, He will simultaneously use you to sharpen the gifts in others. We find this principle in the book of Proverbs: "As iron sharpens iron, so a friend sharpens a friend" (Proverbs 27:17 *NLT*).

Through his role as the "go-to" Bible teacher in the church of Antioch, Saul learned how to effectively communicate the connection between the Old and New Covenants. Living and ministering in Antioch's diverse environment was also strategic to his developing understanding of God's vision of the Church and what it meant to be a *new man* in Christ (*see* 2 Corinthians 5:17).

In Antioch, blacks, whites, Jews, and Gentiles all mingled together in leadership and worship. This was something that had never existed before. God used the plethora of nationalities and cultures represented in the congregation to give Saul a broad perspective of the Gospel and its mission and to paint a powerful picture of what the Church should look like — a colorful tapestry of people from all walks of life. Through the death, burial, and resurrection of Jesus Christ, God was creating one new man — the Body of Christ. The wall separating Jews and Gentiles had been broken down and destroyed, and salvation was equally available to all of mankind.

> God will use your environment — the people, places, and opportunities around you — to shape and sharpen your gifts. And while He is in the process of developing your gifts, He will simultaneously use you to sharpen the gifts in others.

Saul lived and breathed this truth every day as he rubbed elbows with people from different cultures who were saved and filled with the Holy Ghost. Just think of what a radical shift in thinking this was for him! Saul, a Hebrew of Hebrews, "circumcised on the eighth day," was worshiping and working side by side with uncircumcised people from different ethnic groups and backgrounds who had made Jesus Christ their Lord and Savior.

Saul saw with his own eyes the power of God working in and through people from all nations. How could he argue with a Greek being saved? How could he argue with an African being a leader in the church? All of this was happening right in front of him. In fact, people of diverse backgrounds were serving alongside Saul as elders in the church and functioning as prophets and teachers. It was a new revelation of the new man in Christ — not from one blood or one nation, but from *many*. This was a radical idea!

It was from this revelation that the apostle would later write:

> **For you are all children of God through faith in Christ Jesus. And all who have been united with Christ in baptism have put on Christ, like putting on new clothes. There is no longer Jew or Gentile, slave or free, male and female. For you are all one in Christ Jesus.**
>
> **Galatians 3:26-28** *NLT*

This insight is one of the core foundational truths of the New Testament. However, it is doubtful that Paul ever would have understood that in Jerusalem the way he grasped it in Antioch. He had to be placed in the environment at Antioch in order to be equipped and prepared.

ALLOW GOD TO EQUIP AND PREPARE YOU

When I look at my life, I see that God has always put me in the right place to prepare me for my next step. For example, before Denise and I began our teaching ministry many years ago, God placed me under a pastor who taught the Word with great depth and authority, pulling insight from the original Greek text of the New Testament. Over the course of several years, I worked under this pastor as his assistant, during which time he taught me discipline and how to dedicate my mind to the serious study of the Word. God used that Bible-rich environment to prepare Denise and me for our teaching ministry, and this godly man's influence continues to impact our lives and ministry today.

When Denise and I began traveling and teaching all over America in the early days of our ministry, we made dear friends with pastors from across the country who would later support us when we moved to the USSR. At the time, we had no idea that those men and women of God and their congregations would become our financial lifeline when we later pursued the call of God overseas. But if we hadn't traveled and cultivated those relationships in those early years, we wouldn't have had the connections to support God's next huge assignment for our lives.

Being in the right place at the right time is vital to your preparation!

So what environment are you in? Are you where *God* placed you in the Body of Christ (*see* 1 Corinthians 12:18) — or are you just where *you* want to be?

Remember, God knows what you need and is working a plan to fully develop the gifts He has placed in you. However, you have to allow Him to place you in the environment He knows is best.

> **God knows what you need and is working a plan to fully develop the gifts He has placed in you. However, you have to allow Him to place you in the environment He knows is best.**

It might be that God has asked you to go somewhere and you have struggled with it. You've asked, *Lord, why in the world would You take me there?* But never forget that the Bible teaches: "Man's steps are ordered by the Lord. How then can a man understand his way?" (Proverbs 20:24 *AMPC*).

Maybe the church where you're located right now is your "Holy Spirit University," just as Antioch was for Paul. For instance, it could be God's training ground for you to learn how to submit to authority and serve others. That doesn't mean it will be easy on your flesh, but just be still and know that He is God (*see* Psalm 46:10). It may not be your final destination, but perhaps it is a needed step for you to fulfill your destiny.

Perhaps the environment you're living in has so much mental noise and clutter that you don't think you can hear what God is saying. Rest assured — the Holy Spirit is working in you to find the solution, because He wants you to hear His voice even more than you desire it. Once again, this could be your spiritual training ground for the crucial days ahead. You need to learn the art of getting quiet on the inside, even in the midst of chaotic circumstances and external noise, so you can discern accurately what the Holy Spirit is trying to get across to you.

Or you might think the negative influence of the people around you — or what you *perceive* is negative — is hindering you from developing your gifts. That can definitely be a very uncomfortable situation, but it doesn't mean God hasn't placed you there. That is a vital lesson to learn, and it will serve you well when it's time to transition into a season of greater responsibility in His plan for your life.

Another possibility is that you might be too comfortable where you are at in this particular phase of your life. Your comfort zone may be hindering you from having to stretch and totally depend on God. If so, you might begin to sense a "divine discomfort" growing as the Lord prepares you to say *yes* to His call to "step out of the boat" and follow Him into a new place of challenge and purpose. Or it may be that you simply need to spend time before the Lord renewing your commitment to depend solely on Him in all things — not your paycheck, your friends, or your familiar surroundings. That way you'll always be ready for the next step, whatever it may be, in His plan for you.

Whatever the case, it's vital that you stay open and allow God to place you where He desires. And just as you trust the Lord to set you in place according to His will, you must also trust Him to *work in you* while you are in that place so you can learn and develop in every area of your life the way He intends. The right environment is a major key to finding and fulfilling His will for your life. In fact, it's *critical*!

> Just as you trust the Lord to set you in place according to His will, you must also trust Him to *work in you* while you are in that place so you can learn and develop in every area of your life the way He intends.

I encourage you to open your heart to the Lord so He can reveal and remove any wrong attitudes. Don't be afraid to obey Him. He's not going to hurt you or mislead you. He's working on *equipping* you for success! If you endeavor to always be where He wants you to be with a willing, obedient heart — just as Paul was in Antioch for that season — God will use your experiences to prepare you for the next step of your life.

Just determine to yield to that process of divine preparation. Be flexible and pliable like a perfectly conditioned wineskin, joyfully receiving the new wine of His Spirit. Allow His Word to dwell richly in your life, and submit yourself to the leaders He has placed over you. You will find that by doing so, God will bring you into the fullness of His will, and you will ultimately see your personal divine assignment through to completion.

Think About It

1. Being in the right physical environment is a major key to developing your gifts. Take a moment to briefly describe the environment in which you live. This would include your church, place of work, and community. In what ways is it "exploding with life"? Conversely, in what ways is it causing you to dig deep into your commitment to follow God's leading, no matter what? How does it challenge and motivate you to serve God willingly and obediently and how is He using it to help develop your gifts?

2. After reading this chapter, what is the Holy Spirit speaking to you? Are you in the environment where you know you need to be? If not, what actions do you sense the Lord prompting you to take? Get quiet and hear His heart. Write what He reveals.

3. How would you describe yourself — as a dry, stretched-out old wineskin, or as a new wineskin that is open and flexible to receive the flow of the Holy Spirit? What evidence in your life confirms that you are spiritually flexible?

4. Are you in a place where God can prepare you for the exact task He has called you to do? If not, or if you are unsure, have you sought the Lord to find out where He wants to place you so you can become equipped for the next phase He has planned for your life?

5. Can you think of a person, church, or organization that was once pliable in the hands of the Holy Spirit but became stiff and inflexible over a period of time? What have you learned by observing that process about what *you* need to do to avoid becoming an old wineskin that becomes less usable in the hands of God?

CHAPTER THREE

WHEN GOD FINALLY LAUNCHES YOU, *STAY ON TRACK*!

*E*ventually a moment comes for you to launch out into God's plan for your life — a watershed moment that unequivocally changes *everything*. That moment becomes a pivotal point in your life journey that separates you from your past and thrusts you onto a path that leads to the future God has for you. And if you faithfully stick with the plan He has shown you, your obedience will open the way for supernatural power, provision, and protection to become a living reality in your life. It's an exciting adventure you'll never regret!

Saul had just such a watershed moment in Antioch, and it changed the course of his life. After serving alongside other leaders in the church at Antioch for a number of years, we can safely conclude that Saul was eager to get started in his own ministry, even as he waited for God's perfect timing. You could say he was like a huge jumbo jet sitting on the runway — fueled up, ready to fly, and just waiting for the Lord to say, "Now is the time to get going!"

Then one day when the leaders of the Antioch church were praying together, a prophetic word was spoken that literally hurled Saul into God's plan for his life. Acts 13:2,3 relates that landmark moment:

> **As they ministered to the Lord, and fasted, the Holy Ghost said, Separate me Barnabas and Saul for the work whereunto I have called them. And when they had fasted and prayed, and laid their hands on them, they sent them away.**

With this one directive from the Holy Spirit, Saul was launched into his calling. The year was approximately 45 AD — about eight years after he'd had an encounter with the Lord on the road to Damascus and several years since he had first arrived in Antioch. After proving himself faithful during those years of preparation in Antioch, Saul had arrived at the golden moment for his dream to be birthed. With this clear word from Heaven, the leaders in Antioch laid hands on Saul, and he stepped out in faith to begin his apostolic ministry with Barnabas at his side. From this pivotal moment on, Scripture also indicates that Saul was called Paul.

STICK WITH THE PLAN
GOD GAVE YOU

In Chapter One, we saw that when Ananias prayed for Saul in Damascus at the time of his conversion, Ananias delivered a prophetic word that God had given him concerning Saul's life. In that prophetic word, Jesus had told Ananias that Saul was "…a chosen vessel unto me, to bear my name before the *Gentiles*, and *kings*, and the *children of Israel*" (Acts 9:15).

I want you to notice the explicit order of Saul's divine call in this list:

- First and foremost, Saul was to take the message of Christ to the Gentiles.

- Secondarily, Saul was to represent Christ to kings and to governmental authorities.

- Third, and lastly, Saul was to take Christ to the children of Israel.

This list was God's way of defining priorities in His call on Saul's life. Saul's first and primary call, higher and above all others, was to reach the Gentile world with the message of Jesus Christ. Second on the list, and given as a secondary priority, Saul was to be God's spokesman before kings and governmental authorities. Third and last in terms of priority, Saul was to bear witness of Christ to the children of Israel.

But what happened when Saul — who from that point on was called Paul — actually launched out into his apostolic ministry? A study in the book of Acts of Paul's early years of ministry seems to indicate that instead of putting the Gentiles first, which was God's plan for his life, Paul apparently tried to put the Jews *first* and the Gentiles *last*. Paul's veering from the original plan may be the reason he experienced so much frustration and minimal fruitfulness in the earliest years of his apostolic ministry. Several times Paul was run out of town by groups of angry Jews who not only didn't want to hear what he had to say, but who also wanted to harm him. (*see* Acts 13:50; 14:5,6; 17:5,13,14).

It seems good to point out here that some interpret Paul's decision to approach the Jews first differently than what I have stated. People holding this view consider Paul's early methods as more strategic and intentional. In other words, they believe that Paul sought to reach as many Jews and God-fearers as he could in order to establish a base from which he could then have a more effective outreach to the Gentiles.

Those who come from this perspective speculate that Paul was perhaps using the Jews whom he reached initially in a given city so he could prepare to be even more effective when he did turn his attention to the Gentiles. They attribute the logic of this perspective to God's strategy in the overall plan of salvation. God used the Jewish people as the platform from which to offer the Messiah, whose plan of redemption then went out to reach the whole world.

I understand the point that those who hold this view are endeavoring to make, but I'll explain why I believe that the most reasonable conclusion to make, given the full testimony of the Scriptures, is that Paul's ministry did not initially reflect the prophetic order of priorities that Jesus revealed to him in Acts 9:15.

Taking up the discussion again of my personal conclusion regarding Paul's early years of ministry, let me stress the valuable personal lesson you can glean from a study of this aspect of this apostle's walk with God. One of the vital keys to your success on this earth is to know the will of God for your life and then to stick closely to what He has revealed to you. If you hold fast to the plan as God gave it to you, you position yourself to access a continual supply of His power, provision, and protection.

> **One of the vital keys to your success on this earth is to know the will of God for your life and then to stick closely to what He has revealed to you.**

Of course, your obedience to God doesn't guarantee you a trouble-free life. For one thing, Paul himself wrote, "Yea, and all that will live godly in Christ Jesus shall suffer persecution" (2 Timothy 3:12). You will always have to stay alert to thwart the attacks of an enemy who continually looks for ways to derail or discourage you as you seek to fulfill what God has asked you to do. And as you pursue the assignment He has given you, the threat of calamity or danger can never be the measuring rod of your obedience to His plan for your life.

But the fact remains that you can open yourself up to unnecessary attacks when you veer from what God has revealed to you regarding His priorities for your life. And as a result of deviating from pursuing His plan for you *His* way, you may experience a lack of His power, provision, or protection in ways you never would have if you'd been careful to stick closely not only to what He told you to do, but also *how* He told you to do it.

It's true that Paul endured some level of persecution throughout the course of his ministry. It's also true that he was eventually martyred as a result of standing true to Christ. But a study of his ministry reveals that after Paul positioned himself correctly in his divine priorities and began to focus on ministering to the Gentiles, he eventually experienced a phenomenal level of provision and protection.

Paul even experienced a level of divine protection in death, although that may be difficult for the Western mind to comprehend. Most of those who were arrested at that time for similar reasons were horrifically burned at the stake or endured the grueling death of crucifixion. In contrast, Paul's status as a Roman citizen positioned him by Roman law to a quick, expedient death rather than a prolonged, painful one, sparing him a torturous end.

I feel it necessary at this juncture to acknowledge that during certain periods of time in certain parts of the world, many believers, past and present, have suffered and do suffer to the point of death for their faith. We must remember Jesus' words: "…In the world you will have tribulation: but be of good cheer; I have overcome the world" (John 16:33).

Escaping trouble was never promised in Scripture, but experiencing the overcoming power and presence of God is promised to those who trust Him as they hold fast to His revealed will for their lives. Times may be difficult, but those who stay on track and refuse to budge from their divinely assigned place will encounter the presence of God's power to sustain and undergird them, no matter what they face.

If you walk out God's plan *your* way, you may enjoy a measure of success, but it will be nothing compared to what you would have experienced if you had stayed with the original plan as He revealed it to you. If you want supernatural power, miraculous provision, and divine protection to be a continued reality in your life journey, you must make sure at all times that *you are where God wants you to be and you're doing what He has told you to do.*

I encourage you to evaluate your walk with God in light of these questions:

- Have I stayed true to the plan God gave me?

- Have I veered in any way from the assignment that I know God has given me to complete?

- Have I enjoyed the power, provision, and protection that I know is mine in Christ as I've pursued God's plan for my life?

- Have I experienced a measure of the success that I've dreamed about and that I know God wants to give to me?

If you are frustrated with your Christian life and have wondered why you haven't walked in a higher level of victory, I ask you to carefully contemplate what you are about to read in the rest of this chapter with an open mind and heart. I want you to see from Scripture what happens when a believer deviates from the plan God has for his life. I also want you to see how quickly blessings will return to that believer as he realigns himself with God's original plan.

DON'T MAKE THE MISTAKE OF 'DEFAULTING' TO YOUR COMFORT ZONE

Paul would have naturally felt comfortable with Jews because he was himself a Jew. So Paul could have been tempted to follow his natural tendency to go where he felt most comfortable — instead of keeping his priorities in divine order. This "defaulting" to one's comfort zone is a mistake that has been made by multitudes of believers through the centuries. And, regardless of who the person is, it always yields the same frustrating results as Paul apparently experienced in the early years of his ministry.

Going where you feel comfortable and being where God wants you to be are often two separate things that don't coincide with each other. You may have heard people incorrectly say, "God will never call you where you are not comfortable." Forgive me for being so blunt, but it doesn't take too much deep thinking to realize that statement is totally out of sync with biblical reality.

> Going where you feel comfortable and being where God wants you to be are often two separate things that don't coincide with each other.

If that "stay where you're comfortable" mentality had been embraced by the Christians of the First Century, it is questionable whether you or I would know Jesus Christ as our Lord and Savior today. We heard the Gospel and responded to its truth in *our* generation because early believers were willing to be the first to go where they were *not* comfortable to bring the Gospel to the lost — people just like you and me. We are the fruit of those courageous early

Christians venturing beyond their comfort zones to go where they never dreamed they would go and to reach a people they never knew they would reach. It was their willingness to step out so long ago that is ultimately why you and I know the Lord today.

The Bible is *filled* with people whom God called to places and to people who were not naturally "comfortable" to them.

If you have bought into this fictional way of thinking — that God calls you only to places and situations where you're comfortable — you can kiss adventures in God good-bye, because they will never be yours. You'll never go far from your little neighborhood or your small circle of friends. That kind of thinking will stop you from reaching nations, achieving dreams, or moving mountains by faith.

To do the impossible, you must be willing to stretch — and that means being willing to go to places that are totally unknown to you and to people to whom you are not naturally drawn. It may sound scary, but God's grace will empower you to do it *if* you're willing to say *yes* and obey!

> If you have bought into this fictional way of thinking — that God calls you only to places and situations where you're comfortable — you can kiss adventures in God good-bye, because they will never be yours.

By studying the book of Acts, you will easily get the impression that the apostle Paul found it very difficult to venture outside his Jewish comfort zone to become immersed in the Gentile world. Being reared a Jew in a strict Jewish community, Paul had grown up with a totally different worldview from the Gentiles. The Gentile world was pagan, and Paul would have been naturally repelled by many of their practices, lifestyles, and behaviors. In fact, to separate himself from such people and practices was a *requirement* of his Jewish upbringing!

For all of these reasons, we can surmise that the prospect of going to the Gentiles first and foremost with the Gospel, as the Holy Spirit had clearly commanded, was *not* Paul's preference. Studying the book of Acts, we discover repeated examples of times when Paul went to a new city and was drawn like a magnet to the city synagogue. Time after time, he was tempted to go where he felt most at ease, comfortable, and at home — that is, to the local Jewish community.

But as much as Paul longed to reach the Jews first with the Gospel, he was most often met with Jewish disdain, rejection, and hostility in nearly all these instances. It didn't matter that Paul was a Jew — most of his Jewish audience didn't want to hear what he had to say. As a result, only a limited amount of fruit was reaped among Paul's Jewish listeners.

In contrast, the Gentiles who happened to hear Paul preach during those early years were often openhearted and receptive. They would even beg to hear more of his unique message.

It would be fair to say Paul's attempts to reach the Jewish community in those early years of apostolic ministry were repeatedly beleaguered with frustration and minimal fruit. On the other hand, Paul's somewhat inadvertent ministry at times to Gentiles seemed to abound with the fruit of people won into the Kingdom and of other supernatural results.

The fruit produced among the Gentiles was simply off the charts compared to the results Paul regularly experienced with his Jewish audience. The Gentiles' hearts were open and curious, and they *wanted* to hear what this man had to say. Nonetheless, for several years Paul didn't invest his main energies into ministering to the Gentiles. Instead, he continued to try to reach the Jewish community first with the Gospel because he loved his people so deeply.

One obvious turning point occurred in Paul's ministry after approximately five years of seemingly beating his head against a wall in his attempts to reach the Jewish community. While in Corinth, Paul became so exasperated with the negative response he received from the Jews of the city that he finally declared: "…Your blood be upon your own heads; I am clean; from henceforth I will go unto the Gentiles"!

Verse 7 goes on to say, "And he departed thence, and entered into a certain man's house, named Justus, one that worshipped God, whose house joined hard to the synagogue."

Paul had finally abandoned his attempts to make Jews his first priority and turned to the Gentile world as his primary focus — which had been God's revealed desire for him all along. And when the apostle got on track with the original plan, God's blessings on his ministry immediately began to abound with striking results.

Acts 18:8 records the great favor Paul found among the Gentiles of Corinth when he turned his attention to them — as well as the favor he found with a few strategic members of the Jewish community: "…Crispus, the chief ruler of the synagogue, believed on the Lord with all his house; and many of the Corinthians hearing believed, and were baptized." When Paul got in the right place, focusing on the right thing, he found that at times, he even found favor with some of the Jews!

> When the apostle got on track with the original plan, God's blessings on his ministry immediately began to abound with striking results.

There is a lesson in this for all of us. The Bible lets us know that we can expect to experience persecution at times as a result of obeying God's will. However, we can also know that we will find an increasing level of favor and success as we surrender fully and commit ourselves to doing what the Lord has asked us to do.

Acts 18:8 tells us that many "Corinthians" believed as they listened to Paul's message of the Gospel. These were Gentiles who converted to Christ as the apostle intentionally focused on preaching to them. And in actuality, the Gentile world is where Paul primarily found favor from the beginning of his ministry, even though that audience was probably not his natural preference.

WHAT WERE THE RESULTS?

In our discussion so far, we have seen that for several years, Paul struggled with his desire to try to reach the Jews first and foremost. Then came the pivotal moment when he yielded to the primary call on his life and transferred his focus to ministering to the Gentile world. That decision was a breakthrough moment in Paul's ministry, launching the greatest fruit-producing season in his life.

I'm reminded of a personal testimony shared by a well-known minister that somewhat parallels this pivotal moment of complete alignment to God's call in Paul's life. After this minister had pastored for a significant number of years, the Lord told him that he was at last about to step into the *very first* phase of ministry that He had called him to fulfill! The minister protested when he first heard that, not wanting to believe that those earlier years of pastoring didn't even constitute a phase of his ministry in God's eyes. But the Lord answered, *"I never called you to pastor to begin with."*

It wasn't that this minister was in disobedience or entirely out of the will of God during those years of pastoring. And certainly those years helped equip and prepare the minister for a more targeted focus of pursuing his true calling in the days ahead. But the fact remains that from the Lord's point of view, the beginning of the first phase of ministry did not start until that focus became an applied reality in that minister's walk with God.

As we survey Paul's life, we can see this same principle in demonstration. When Paul realigned himself with the original plan God had given him, he received a greater measure of power and a new impartation of divine protection. He also received miraculous financial provision to pay for his ministry (*see* 2 Corinthians 11:9). It becomes apparent that divine power, protection, and provision specifically manifested when Paul positioned himself within the order of priority God had revealed and assigned to his life years earlier.

When a person is off course to any degree from God's revealed will, his or her results will be commensurately off course as well. Let's look at some instances of how this held true during the early years of ministry when Paul kept taking the Gospel message to the Jews as a first priority.

> **When a person is off course to any degree from God's revealed will, his or her results will be commensurately off course as well.**

From a logical point of view, one may infer that Paul's pattern to first reach the Jewish community was intentional and calculated. For example, as I mentioned earlier, some contend that Paul may have thought the best strategy would be to build a base within the Jewish community with whom he had a common bond, and then from that platform, to begin reaching the Gentiles. But even if this was indeed Paul's intended strategy, the book of Acts reveals that the fruit resulting from his attempts to reach the Jewish community with the Gospel was primarily sparse.

In the city of Salamis on the island of Cyprus, the Jews walked out of the synagogue as Paul was ministering (*see* Acts 13:42). As a result of putting his primary focus on the wrong people in the wrong place, the initial results of Paul's ministry in that city were disappointing. But at the same time, he repeatedly saw that the Gentiles wanted to hear more and even gathered in great numbers to listen to and receive what he had to say.

Not only did the Jews walk out of the synagogue in Salamis, but they also began to blaspheme and verbally fight with Paul and Barnabas in front of the entire town. Filled with envy, these Jews created a stir of riotous proportions that eventually ended in Paul and Barnabas being run out of town.

That was the first time Paul said, "…We turn to the Gentiles" (Acts 13:46). I believe that was an early attempt on the apostle's part to go in the right direction, soon after they were sent out from the Antioch church. However, that intention wasn't fully realized until later when Paul had his "breakthrough moment" in Corinth (*see* Acts 18:6). This early incident with hostile Jews and Paul's response to it gives us a sign that the Holy Spirit was working on Paul's heart from the beginning of his apostolic ministry to show him that his primary grace was in ministering to Gentiles and not to Jews.

> **The Holy Spirit was working on Paul's heart from the beginning of his apostolic ministry to show him that his primary grace was in ministering to Gentiles and not to Jews.**

After shaking the dust off their feet in exasperation in Salamis, the two apostles moved on to the next city — Iconium. Once again, where did Paul and Barnabas immediately go when they arrived in this new city? They went to the synagogue. And once again, what was the response they received? The apostles found almost no favor among the Jewish listeners, who for the most part rejected their message.

Acts 14:2 says, "But the unbelieving Jews stirred up the Gentiles, and made their minds evil affected against the brethren." This time the stir resulted in "...an *assault* made both of the Gentiles, and also of the Jews with their rulers, to use them despitefully, and to stone them" (Acts 14:5).

The Greek word for *assault* means *to rush forward*. A stampede of angry people rushed forward to try to beat, stone, and destroy Paul and Barnabas, but the two apostles fled for their lives and went south to Lystra and Derbe.

In these two new cities, the apostolic team once again found great favor with the Gentiles, who readily received the message. In fact, there was such an outward demonstration of God's power among them that the Gentiles in their ignorance actually thought Paul and Barnabas were the Greek gods Mercury and Jupiter who had come down from the heavens!

Finally, Paul was beginning to reach out to the right people and, as a result, experience great success. The Gentiles had opened their hearts, witnessed the power of God in demonstration, and acknowledged His awesomeness. Everything was going great — until the unbelieving Jews from Antioch and Iconium showed up and stirred up another riot. In the end, these hostile Jews stoned Paul in Lystra, and God had to supernaturally raise him up (*see* Acts 14:19,20). This was the kind of reception and treatment Paul repeatedly endured at the hands of those Jews who were vehemently opposed to his message of the Gospel.

We see later in Paul's second epistle to the Corinthians that this incessant persecution he endured from hostile Jews in his ministry was not entirely avoidable, even after he aligned himself more fully with the Lord's priorities in his divine call. Paul alluded

to this unrelenting opposition as "a thorn in the flesh" in Second
Corinthians 12:7-9:

> …There was given to me a thorn in the flesh, the mes-
> senger of Satan to buffet me, lest I should be exalted above
> measure. For this thing I besought the Lord thrice, that it
> might depart from me. And he said unto me, My grace is suf-
> ficient for thee: for my strength is made perfect in weakness.
> Most gladly therefore will I rather glory in my infirmities,
> that the power of Christ may rest upon me.

The "thorn in the flesh" might include the jealous, false
apostles who would follow Paul, trying to discredit his ministry
(*see* 2 Corinthians 11:13-15). However, it is likely that Paul was
also referring to these groups of malevolent Jews who harassed
him throughout his missionary journeys. He couldn't fully get rid
of them, so he had to depend on God's grace to deal with them.

Stay the Course
God Has Put You On

Whether your "watershed moment" has arrived or you are still
on the launching pad, there *are* specific things that you know
God has instructed you to do. The question is this: *Are you following through on what you know to do?*

Paul had been called, equipped, and prepared by God. He had
been given a specific assignment to bring the light of the Gospel
to the Gentiles *first*, then to kings, and lastly to the children of
Israel. But somehow it seems he confused the priorities of God's
will for his life and, as a result, suffered unnecessary frustration
and limited fruit for the Kingdom for a period of time.

There is strength and success in staying the course God puts
you on. That's not to say that you will never suffer any hardship,

but many trials and hardships can be avoided simply by living a life of obedience. As the psalmist prayed thousands of years ago, we, too, can pray today:

> **Teach me your decrees, O Lord; I will keep them to the end. Give me understanding and I will obey your instructions; I will put them into practice with all my heart. Make me walk along the path of your commands, for that is where my happiness is found.**
>
> **Psalm 119:33-35** *NLT*

Friend, *stay the course* God has placed you on, and don't deviate from His instructions. Let Him be the One to move you or adjust your assignment. Be willing to work hard to accomplish His will, and thank Him for the people He has teamed you with to encourage you and lighten your load.

> **There is strength and success in staying the course God puts you on.**

If you have made mistakes and gotten off course, repent and receive God's forgiveness — and then correct your course. As you obey God's call on your life, the fullness of His will is sure to produce lasting, abundant fruit. You have His unfailing Word on it!

THINK ABOUT IT

1. When you're still in the midst of the preparation and equipping process, waiting to be launched can feel wearisome. But don't despair or try to move prematurely. *Pray* and ask God for His grace to stay put and learn what you need to learn so you will be ready for your launch date. Write down anything He is speaking to you right now so you don't forget later and deviate from the course He has set you on.

2. Each of us has our own unique place of ministry in the Body of Christ. Do you know whom God has specifically called you to minister to? If so, who is it and in what ways are you endeavoring to faithfully reach out to these people?

3. Paul experienced many hardships at the hands of unbelieving Jews. Had he gone to the Gentiles first as Jesus had instructed, it is possible that he would have been more successful earlier in his ministry and avoided a great deal of the hardship he encountered early on.

   Get quiet before the Lord and ask Him to show you your heart. Ask Him: "Have I done anything to deviate from Your call on my life? Have my priorities gotten mixed up along the way? Am I experiencing hardship because I haven't fully obeyed You?" Be still and listen to what He reveals. Write down and carry out any actions He prompts you to take.

CHAPTER FOUR

GETTING INTO GOD'S WILL CAN BE A PROCESS — DON'T GIVE UP!

*A*re you struggling to get yourself in line with what you know God's will is for your life? You're in good company. The Bible is filled with people who had come to know the will of God, but who experienced a prolonged "in-between time" while everything came into alignment so His divine plan could be realized in their lives.

Consider Abram (later called Abraham). He heard from God, but it took him decades to fully experience what God had promised him (*see* Genesis chapters 12-21). Joseph had a dream from the Lord about rising to a place of great authority and position, but it took him more than a decade to fully walk in that call on his life (*see* Genesis chapters 37, 39-41).

Likewise, David was anointed of God to be king of Israel years in advance of his actually stepping into that role. David spent many years first serving *under* King Saul and then running for his life *from* the king before his calling *to be* the king became a reality (*see* 1 Samuel chapters 16-31; 2 Samuel chapters 1-2).

Each of these men — Abraham, Joseph, and David — experienced times of confusion, discouragement, and frustration as they went through the process of getting fully aligned with God's will for their lives.

And the same can be true in each of our lives. Sometimes it takes awhile for us to really understand what God is saying. We discern His leading in our hearts, but for various reasons, we don't understand with our intellects what He's actually saying to us. Sometimes the timing doesn't seem right; at other times, our own wrong mindsets or selfish preferences can hinder our understanding. Or perhaps we understand generally what God is saying to us, but we need to press on in prayer to discern the specifics He wants us to grasp.

In this chapter, we will focus on the apostle Paul and learn why it took him approximately five years to get fully aligned and in place according to the pattern God had ordained for him. As we go through each section, determine whether you can see yourself in the examples presented, including the example from my own life.

As you will see, sometimes it takes awhile for us to really understand or fully embrace what God wants to do in our lives. Perhaps we hear His voice in our hearts, but our emotions don't want to accept what He's saying. As a result, we rationalize that God couldn't really be saying what we *think* He is saying to us. At other times, there may be a blockage inside us that hinders our progress — a wrong mindset, a stubborn will — and before we can proceed, that hindrance has to be eliminated by the power of the Spirit.

> Sometimes it takes awhile for us to really understand or fully embrace what God wants to do in our lives.

So let's take a closer look at the example of the apostle Paul and see why it took him a number of years to get fully positioned in pursuit of his divine calling according to God's priorities and plans.

Understanding God's Call
Was a Process for Paul

Knowing the will of God and then deliberately positioning yourself *in* the will of God is the combination that produces the key to success. Just knowing the will of God won't bring you success; you have to know it *and* be in it through your conscious choice to obey what He has asked you to do.

As we discussed in the last chapter, the apostle Paul knew God's will for him. But it seems apparent that Paul had a difficult time embracing the audience God had primarily called him to reach. The Bible doesn't explicitly say that the apostle struggled with fully accepting this aspect of his divine assignment. But when we look at Paul's actions, we can see that it wasn't his natural inclination or preference to make the Gentiles the first priority of his thoughts, prayers, and actions, even though they were the people God had called him to focus on.

> Just knowing the will of God won't bring you success; you have to know it *and* be in it through your conscious choice to obey what He has asked you to do.

We saw in Chapter Three that for the first years after Paul launched out into apostolic ministry, his actions seemed to belie the priorities of his call. We also saw that, by all appearances, he was initially not very successful. God had called Paul to bring the Gospel *first* to the Gentiles, *second* to kings and governments, and *third* to the children of Israel (*see* Acts 9:15). But he kept going to the Jews *first* — and in doing so, he was putting his primary focus on the wrong crowd. A study of the journeys of Paul reveals that it was especially during those early years that he experienced intense persecution, minimal fruit, and a deficiency of the funds needed to be in full-time ministry.

Why did it take Paul several years before he fully aligned himself with the call to focus on reaching the Gentile world with the Gospel? There seems to be three primary reasons that explain why he went through a process that led him to that critical point.

REASON #1
PAUL WAS A JEW — INSIDE AND OUT

Paul was called to the Gentiles, but he was a Jew inside and out. Paul was "circumcised the eighth day, of the stock of Israel, of the tribe of Benjamin, an Hebrew of the Hebrews; as touching the law, a Pharisee" (Philippians 3:5). Paul perceived everything through Jewish eyes. He had been raised in a strict, orthodox Jewish home, and he had a very Jewish understanding of life, faith, and Scripture. He hadn't grown up being schooled in the ways of the Gentiles, but what he did know of their world was *not* attractive to him.

The pagan Gentile world had a very different culture than the one Paul was accustomed to. He had grown up worshiping the one true God, whereas pagans worshiped numerous gods. They were uncircumcised idol worshipers whose lands were filled with drunkenness, debauchery, and multiple forms of sexual immorality.

Can you imagine what Paul — then called Saul — might have been thinking as he tried to grasp what Jesus had told him? *I'm a Jew, and these Gentiles are morally filthy. How am I supposed to connect with them? Why in the world would a Jewish man like me want to live among all these heathen nations?* Saul's mind must have been going *"tilt, tilt, tilt!"* But in his heart, he knew God had called him to reach the Gentile world.

This internal tug-of-war between Paul's spirit and soul must have been a very real struggle for him in the early years of his ministry. That he was called to the Gentiles had been confirmed over and over — but the apostle's soul naturally gravitated toward the Jews. To instead focus on the Gentiles and connect with them from his heart was a huge leap of faith for Paul. In the end, it would take approximately five years for him to fully engage this aspect of his call and to adjust his life accordingly.

REASON #2
PAUL WAS COMFORTABLE

Another major reason it took Paul a number of years to fully embrace his call to the Gentiles was the *comfort factor*. As I said previously, Paul naturally gravitated toward the Jews in every city he went to because of his strict Jewish upbringing. The synagogue was his familiar "comfort zone," and his preference for that environment was undoubtedly not an easy thing to shake.

Paul knew the customs and culture of the Jews by heart, and he understood innately how Jewish people thought. In Antioch, this knowledge had set him apart and made him shine among the leaders. Connecting with the Gentile world was new, and "new" is often scary and intimidating. The whole thought of associating closely with the uncircumcised must have initially made Paul feel very uneasy.

The truth is, I have met very few people who enjoy change. We all like to be where we feel comfortable, and our flesh naturally gravitates to what is easy. It seems so effortless to take the path of least resistance. We are drawn to what is familiar and will usually shy away from anything that will "rock our boat."

For Paul, his early experiences of going to the Gentiles with the message of the Gospel might be likened to what it's like for the new kid at school. Coming into that foreign setting would have required a great deal of change for Paul. It was crucial that he learn the cultural norms and mindsets within the new environment so he'd know how to communicate with these people who were so completely different than him.

> I have met very few people who enjoy change. We all like to be where we feel comfortable, and our flesh naturally gravitates to what is easy. It seems so effortless to take the path of least resistance.

Paul in his heart had said *yes* to God, yet it seems that for a period of time, he still had a mindset that kept directing him to the Jews. But whether or not the apostle felt comfortable ministering to the Gentiles, God's will was for him to do just that. Paul's preferences, desires, and level of comfort had to take a back seat to God's plan. The same is true for you and me.

Here's the good news! If God is asking you to do something that is totally out of your comfort zone and contrary to your way of thinking, He will change your thoughts to become agreeable to His will. You'll find the path to this desired outcome in Proverbs 16:3 (*AMPC*):

> **Roll your works upon the Lord [commit and trust them wholly to Him;** *He will cause your thoughts to become agreeable to His will,* **and] so shall your plans be established and succeed.**

What a powerful promise from God — *He will cause your thoughts to become agreeable to His will, and your plans shall succeed because they are HIS plans.* But it isn't automatic — there is something you must do first. You must commit your way wholly and completely to Him.

Eventually Paul did just that, and God was then able to create a *new* "comfort zone" in his life — one that was filled with Gentiles and in which multitudes responded to the message of God's saving grace through Jesus Christ.

REASON #3
PAUL WAS BURDENED FOR THE JEWS

The third reason — and I believe the most significant — Paul had a difficult time making the Gentiles his top priority was his overwhelming burden for his own countrymen. Remember, Paul was a Jew inside and out. He loved the Jewish people passionately and wanted to see them saved.

Paul's heart for the Jews is clearly revealed in the words he wrote in Romans 1:16: "For I am not ashamed of the gospel of Christ: for it is the power of God unto salvation to every one that believeth; *to the Jew first*, and also to the Greek."

Being a devout Jew, Paul had an innate desire to reach his own people first with the message of the Gospel and prevent them from going to hell. No one wants his or her own family to spend eternity in hell.

> Being a devout Jew, Paul had an innate desire to reach his own people first with the message of the Gospel and prevent them from going to hell. No one wants his or her own family to spend eternity in hell.

The Jews were the natural, chosen people of God. Abraham, who was their forefather, was the first to receive God's promises, and the Jews were the natural heirs of those promises. Similarly,

Moses was in the Jewish lineage, and he was the first to receive God's commandments. The Jews were the natural heirs of those commandments (*see* Romans 9:4,5).

In light of these truths, it seems only natural that the Jews should have been the first to receive the Gospel. But even so, the Jews were not Paul's primary call; God had given that task to Peter and several of the other apostles. Paul was called to take the message of salvation and forgiveness of sin through Jesus Christ to the Gentiles.

Of all the epistles the apostle Paul wrote, no passage of Scripture communicates the depth of his burden for the Jews more clearly than Romans 9:1-3.

> **I say the truth in Christ, I lie not, my conscience also bearing me witness in the Holy Ghost, that I have great heaviness and continual sorrow in my heart. For I could wish that myself were accursed from Christ for my brethren, my kinsmen according to the flesh.**
>
> **Romans 9:1-3**

Notice Paul's phrase in verse 2: "I have great heaviness." The word "great" is the Greek word *mega*, which always speaks of *enlargement*. If a person wants to describe something *huge* but doesn't know exactly how big it is, he would use the word *mega*. It would be just like someone saying, "I have *mega* bills to pay," or, "I have *mega* work to do," or, "I'm dealing with *mega* stress like you wouldn't believe!" *Mega* always describes something *enormous*.

The word "heaviness" is the Greek word *lupe*, and it describes *a deep sorrow in the soul — a sorrow so deep that words cannot express it*. This kind of hurt is like *a severe sickness* or *a festering sore that never gets well*.

When we combine the original meanings of these two words, this phrase could be translated as Paul saying, *"I have a hurt so deep, a sorrow so severe, that it's like a sore that never heals or gets better. It's a sickness in my heart from which I find no relief."* This is how Paul described his deep burden for the Jewish people.

The next thing Paul said he had in his heart was "continual sorrow." The word "continual" means *no pause; no break;* or *something that never ceases, not even for a second.* And the word "sorrow" would be better translated as *anguish, torment,* or *an all-consuming grief.* This sorrow is *a pain that completely consumes the heart, the mind, and the emotions.*

Those words "anguish" and "torment" are very strong words. When Paul said he had "continual sorrow," he was actually saying he had *incessant torment* about that situation. When we compound the original meanings of "continual sorrow," it is as if Paul was saying, *"I feel a tormenting anguish — an all-consuming sense of pain and grief — from which I never get rest, not even for a moment."*

When we take the original meanings of Paul's entire phrase, "I have great heaviness and continual sorrow of heart," a more expanded interpretation of it could read this way:

> *"I have a hurt so deep and a sorrow so severe that it is like a sore that never heals or gets better; it's a sickness in my heart from which I find no relief. I am tormented constantly with a deep sense of anguish. It's an all-consuming pain and grief from which I never get rest, not even for a moment."*

These words bring into clear focus the most profound reason Paul had such a difficult time making the Gentiles his top priority. He continually carried this overwhelming burden for the Jewish people in his heart.

Paul went on to write something even more profound about this subject: "For I could wish that myself were *accursed* from

Christ for my brethren, my *kinsmen* according to the flesh" (v. 3). The brethren he was talking about are the children of Israel. The word "kinsmen" is the Greek word *sungenes*, which means *of the same genes*. For Paul to say that he wished he could be accursed from Christ so that his kinsmen could be saved meant his burden for them was so incredibly heavy that he was willing to risk even his own salvation for theirs.

When I first read this many years ago, I thought, *Why would Paul make a statement like that? I'd never make a statement like that.* Then I began to dig into the Greek, and I found out that the use of this phrase describes *a wish that cannot be fulfilled.* Therefore, a better translation of this would be, *"If it were possible, I would wish,"* or, *"Of course it's not possible, but I was wishing that if it were possible, I myself could be accursed."*

The word "accursed" is the Greek word *anathema*, which means *appointed to destruction*. So essentially Paul was saying, *"If it were possible — of course it's not, but if it were — I would wish that I could be appointed to destruction if it would result in the salvation of my brethren, my kinsmen, the people I share the same genes with according to the flesh."*

Paul *had* to be filled with the unconditional love of God toward his natural brethren. There is simply no other way anyone could make such a statement. Paul had received a revelation of hell, and he did not want his own kinsmen to go there. When you're filled with the love of God as he was, you will want to do anything you can to keep people you love from going to hell.

For Paul to trade his salvation for the salvation of his people was something he couldn't do — but he was *willing* to do it. As I thought about this, it dawned on me: This is exactly what God did for us through His Son Jesus, who became *accursed* for us to set us free from the curse of the Law (*see* Galatians 3:13)! God the Son became one of us; then He took on all of our sins, sacrificed

Himself, went to hell, and broke Satan's power over us so that we might be saved.

It's important to note that Paul never wrote about the Gentiles the way he wrote about the Jews in Romans 9:1-3. He acknowledged that he was called as an apostle to the Gentiles to preach the Gospel and bear fruit among them. But he never said he was burdened for the Gentiles in the same way he was burdened for the Jewish people.

Of all the reasons that explain why Paul struggled to focus his energies on reaching the Gentiles with the Gospel, his deep burden for the Jewish people is the one that seems to carry the most weight. It was a delayed process for the apostle, but he finally got in a position where he understood the Jews were not to be first in his own ministry, which we'll discuss further in the chapters ahead.

UNDERSTANDING YOUR CALL
MAY ALSO BE A PROCESS

Now you can perhaps see why the sight of a synagogue attracted Paul like a magnet. It wasn't that he wanted to disobey God or be out of His will. Paul just had an overwhelming burden for his kinsmen with whom he shared the same genetics.

Like Paul, you may have found that settling into your divine calling is a process and even a struggle at times. But now you know that you're not alone! Paul struggled. I struggled. And so have many others. So don't feel condemned or discouraged — just join the crowd! Our minds are finite, and sometimes it's difficult for us to comprehend and assimilate what God is saying to us, even if we know it in our hearts.

God may call you to a people or place that you would not naturally choose. He may call you to a church filled with people of a different race and color — an unfamiliar situation you would normally avoid. He may call you to a different city or a different part of the country or to another part of the world, as He called me. Regardless, you can rest assured of this truth: *Wherever God calls you is the best place for you to be!*

> **Like Paul, you may have found that settling into your divine calling is a process and even a struggle at times. But now you know that you're not alone!**

I encourage you to take this opportunity to surrender yourself afresh to do the will of God, no matter what. If your will is strong and if it is opposed to God's will, it may take time for you to come to a place of surrender and total understanding. Just be real with Him and pray this from your heart:

"Lord, I want to hear more clearly from You and to know exactly what You want me to do. What You reveal to me may not be the most natural thing for me to pursue, but I want to desire what *You* want for me. I ask You for Your grace to embrace the place where You have called me to serve. As I do what You are asking, I know I'll experience joy and victory and be fruitful for Your glory. Thank You, Father. In Jesus' name, amen."

THINK ABOUT IT

1. Just about everyone has a dream of some kind. Do you have a dream that you know or sense God has placed in your heart — a call or assignment that He desires to accomplish through you? Is it a struggle for you to accept and believe it? If so, get quiet before the Lord and ask Him to show you why. Write what He reveals, and surrender it to Him in prayer.

2. If you've gotten a glimpse of God's will for your life, can you identify fruit that is being produced from what you know? If not, pray and ask God why not. Do you need to change a certain way of thinking, or do you have a wrong mindset that needs to be removed? Ask Him to reveal any hindrance and to give you His true perspective on the matter.

3. How would you describe your comfort zone? Does it fit with the will of God for your life? If not, pray and ask Him to give you the strength and the desire to align yourself with what He has specifically called you to do in His great plan.

CHAPTER FIVE

DON'T TAKE A DETOUR
FROM GOD'S PLAN

*T*he first step in the process of getting fully aligned with God's will for your life is learning how to hear His voice. But the next step is just as crucial: You must determine you will *fully obey* what you've heard without wavering. Why is that so important? Because many times even when God's call is clear, what He's asking you to do doesn't seem to make sense to your natural mind.

Paul warned us in Romans 8:6 (*AMPC*) regarding the outcome we'll experience if we rely on our own carnal minds rather than follow the Holy Spirit's leading in our lives.

> **Now the mind of the flesh [which is sense and reason *without the Holy Spirit*] is death [death that comprises all the miseries arising from sin, both here and hereafter]. But the mind of the [Holy] Spirit is life and [soul] peace [both now and forever].**

In this verse, Paul described the "mind of the flesh" as *sense and reason without the Holy Spirit* and said that it produces *death* in our lives. God gave each of us a mind to use — but when we lean only on our own understanding instead of trusting in God's Word and the leading of His Spirit, we begin to operate in what Paul called "the mind of the flesh." I have done it; you have done it; and many heroes of the faith have done it. That even includes Abraham, the "father of faith" himself.

> When we lean only on our own understanding instead of trusting in God's Word and the leading of His Spirit, we begin to operate in what Paul called "the mind of the flesh."

Abraham is actually a tremendous biblical example of someone who had to repent for taking detours and then to fully accept God's plan for his life. I realize we are focusing primarily on the life of the apostle Paul in this discussion. But for a few moments, let's look at Abraham's life to see how he also had to learn to follow God's voice and not rely on his own natural understanding.

FOUR DIVINE COMMANDS GIVEN TO ABRAM

We see from Scripture that God gave the same four specific commands twice to Abraham (then called Abram). The first time God spoke to Abram was referred to by Stephen as he stood before the Sanhedrin in Acts 7:2 (*NLT*): "...Our glorious God appeared to our ancestor Abraham in Mesopotamia *before he settled in Haran.*" Then Genesis 12:1 records the second time the Lord gave the same four commands to Abram after he had moved to Haran with his father Terah (*see* Genesis 11:31,32).

> **Now the Lord had said unto Abram, Get thee out of thy country, from thy kindred, from thy father's house, unto a land that I will shew thee.**
>
> **— Genesis 12:1**

What were these four divine commands given to Abram by the Lord? *Number one*, God told Abram to leave his homeland — which was Ur of the Chaldees in Mesopotamia.

Number two, God told Abram to separate himself from all of his relatives — which included his brother Nahor and his nephew Lot, whom he had taken into his home and treated as his own son. Accompanying both men were all their family members, servants, livestock, and possessions.

Number three, Abram was to leave his father Terah's house. Terah was the patriarch of the clan and, as such, would have been held in high regard and deep respect by all in the family, including his own son Abram.

Number four, God said that Abram was to go to the land He would show him. This meant that only Abram and Sarah and their immediate household were called to leave their homeland and travel to an unknown land, trusting the Lord to guide them to their appointed destination.

> Sometimes even simple orders can become complex when man puts his natural mind to them. That's what happened with Abram.

These were the four commands — all of them simple, clear orders — that God gave Abram. But sometimes even simple orders can become complex when man puts his natural mind to interpreting them. That's what happened with Abram.

AFTER HEARING FROM GOD, DON'T RELY ON NATURAL REASONING

The Bible is not explicitly clear on how Abram processed what God had asked him to do. But from what is recorded, we can draw some reasonable conclusions as to what happened.

First, we know from Scripture what God told Abram to do. We also know from Scripture what Abram actually did. It's clear that Abram didn't completely obey the Lord's instructions, possibly because he didn't fully understand what he'd heard God say. In that kind of situation, it's easy for a person to lean to his own understanding and try to figure out things with his own natural reasoning. This is probably what happened in Abram's case.

I can just imagine Abram thinking, *I know that God told me to leave my country with Sarai and to follow Him to a new land that He will show us. I understand His command, and we will do that.*

But as Abram continued to ponder God's words, it is likely that doubts arose. He must have thought, *God told me to leave behind all my relatives. But Lot is like my own son — the son I never had. God couldn't have really intended for me to leave him! And I know God said to leave my father's house, but my father is old and he needs me to take care of him. My father is so respected and beloved by everyone. What will people say about me if I leave him? Lord, You couldn't really have meant for me to leave behind these kinfolk who are so close to me!*

So Abram did *not* leave his homeland with just his own household or immediate family members. Instead, he obeyed according to what he *understood* instead of what he had *heard*. Abram reasoned his way out of some of the divine instructions he had received — and consequently got off course from the very outset regarding what God had commanded him to do.

Abram did only two things *right*: He left his country, and he followed God toward a new land — the *first* and *fourth* instructions God had given him.

What did Abram do that was *contrary* to those divine instructions? He decided to take along Lot and his father Terah, as well as all of their families, servants, flocks, and herds. So when Abram and Sarai left the land of Ur together to head toward an unknown land of promise, they took with them an enormous, over-extended clan by Abram's own choosing. And they only got as far as the city of Haran before Abram's father became ill.

Immediately we can see one reason Abram wasn't supposed to bring Terah. God knows the future, and He knew this was going to happen. Unfortunately, instead of Abram realizing he'd made a mistake and sending Terah back home, Abram decided to camp in the city of Haran and wait for his father either to get well or to die.

Abram's father Terah eventually died from his sickness, and five years later, Abram finally left Haran. When he left the city, the Bible says he and Sarai took with them a massive group of people (*see* Genesis 12:4,5). Imagine all the camels it would require to carry the luggage for the large crowd that traveled with him on this leg of their journey — and how much money it would take to feed and care for them.

What was God's original call to Abram? "You and Sarai leave your country, your relatives, and your father's house, and go to the land I will show you." Abram and Sarai were called to travel to that unknown destination *by themselves* — just the two of them and the servants of their household. But instead, they brought a huge company of people with them, including Lot and his entire entourage. Abram was about to learn that *it doesn't pay to partially obey.*

PARTIAL OBEDIENCE DELAYS GOD'S PLAN

The first five years of Abram's journey became a classic demonstration of a detour that delayed God's perfect plan — all because Abram didn't do everything God had said. Abram was only *partially* obedient, and partial obedience is actually *dis*obedience. God declared through the prophet Isaiah:

> **If you are willing and *obedient*, you shall eat the good of the land.**
>
> **— Isaiah 1:19 *AMPC***

Abram was willing but not fully obedient, and his lack of obedience delayed God's plan several years. It wasn't the devil or the world that delayed His plan; Abram and Sarai *themselves* delayed God's will from coming to pass by not explicitly following His full instructions.

> The first five years of Abram's journey became a classic demonstration of a detour that delayed God's perfect plan — all because Abram didn't do everything God had said. Abram was only *partially* obedient, and partial obedience is actually *dis*obedience.

I've made this mistake in my own life. God has asked me to do certain things, and when I heard His voice, I agreed to do what He said. But afterward, I began to reason within my mind, *Could God really have meant what He said? That just doesn't make much sense. I must not have heard Him right.* Then I added my own interpretation to what God said — and whenever I did that, things got confusing.

Along this line, King Solomon — the wisest king to ever live — wrote this truth:

> **There is a way that *seems right* to a man and *appears straight* before him, but at the end of it is the way of death.**
>
> **Proverbs 16:25 *AMPC***

We cannot follow what *seems* right to us; we must diligently follow what God has actually instructed us to do. Otherwise, we will eventually experience negative consequences, which can include strife, stress, fear, dread, broken relationships, delayed blessings, unfulfilled dreams, and an endless list of other pains and problems.

People often talk about how Abram's great faith sustained him as he stood firm for many years, believing God for His promise to come to pass. But do you think it was God's plan that the fulfillment of Abram's dream would take as long as it did? No. It was God's plan for Abram to fully obey Him the first time and for his dream to come to pass quickly. But because Abram only partially obeyed God's instructions, he misinterpreted God's plan and delayed it from becoming a reality for years.

> We cannot follow what *seems* right to us; we must follow what God has actually instructed us to do.

The good news is that Abram eventually did get back on track. When he did, the plan of God quickly came to pass in his life, and he was blessed.

The bottom line is this: When God speaks to us, we must do *what* He says *the way* He tells us to do it!

PARTIAL OBEDIENCE PRODUCES PROBLEMS

God had mapped out a road for Abram; then He told him how to get on it and follow it. Abram apparently thought he was on the right path, but in reality, he had taken a detour by not carefully obeying God's full instructions. This not only delayed God's plan for Abram, but also produced significant problems in Abram's life.

When Abram and his huge company finally reached the Promised Land, they found themselves in the middle of a severe famine (*see* Genesis 12:10). Of course, God, the Omniscient One, knew beforehand this would take place. If Abram's company had included only himself, Sarai, and their own servants and flocks, they could have stayed in Canaan — the place of blessing to which God had directed them. But with the hordes of people and livestock that Abram had brought with him, there simply wasn't enough food and provision to sustain them all.

We see in this case that even though Abram was in the *right place*, he was connected to the *wrong people* for that divine assignment — and, therefore, he got bumped off course. Since the land could not provide for the needs of all those with him, Abram and his company left Canaan and went down to Egypt in order to survive. Again, the plan of God was delayed.

In Egypt, Abram feared he would be killed and his wife Sarai taken into the Pharaoh's harem because of her beauty. Therefore, Abram convinced Sarai to say that she was his sister so if the Egyptians did take her, at least his life would be spared.

> **Even though Abram was in the *right place*, he was connected to the *wrong people* for that divine assignment — and, therefore, he got bumped off course.**

Sarai actually was Abram's half-sister (*see* Genesis 20:12), but this half-truth was still a lie. When God Himself exposed Abram's plan, Abram was kicked out of Egypt, and he and his entire company traveled back to Canaan (*see* Genesis 12:10-20).

More troubles followed Abram in Canaan — this time concerning his nephew Lot. Both of these men had abundant flocks and herds. In fact, they possessed so much livestock that "...the land could not support both Abram and Lot with all their flocks and herds living so close together" (Genesis 13:6 *NLT*). Abram was a man of peace and had a great love for his nephew, so in parting ways with Lot, he offered him first choice of the land before them (*see* vv. 8,9). Lot chose the land near the cities of Sodom and Gomorrah and pitched his tent there. The rest is history.

Because Abram's decision to take Lot and his company out of Ur with him was contrary to God's instructions, we can conclude that Lot was not where *he* was supposed to be in the years that followed. Lot and his family were later captured as prisoners of war, causing Abram to have to go to war to save them. God gave Abram and his men a miraculous victory, and Lot and his family were rescued. Unfortunately, Lot returned to the city of Sodom and became one of its leading citizens, and his life took a downturn from that point on.

What would have become of Lot had Abram not taken him along? How well might Abram have fared had he and Sarai fully heeded God's instructions and left for the Promised Land alone? Two alternate outcomes seem likely: 1) They all could have avoided many problems and heartaches; and 2) Abram probably could have seen the birth of Isaac a great deal sooner.

> When we obey only the instructions from God that we intellectually understand, we set ourselves up for making mistakes that can have far-reaching consequences.

When we obey only the instructions from God that we intellectually understand, we set ourselves up for making mistakes that can have far-reaching consequences. We need to obey *everything* God tells us to do, even if we don't understand. We must not have the attitude, "Lord, I'll obey You when I understand all the facts." If we wait till we understand everything, we will never obey God.

I'M PERSONALLY FAMILIAR WITH DETOURS

Adding our own interpretation to what we know God has said to us is a very real potential pitfall we must all seek to avoid. When we don't understand our next step, we can easily become anxious and start trying to figure out what we're supposed to do. I can fully relate to this because I've done it a few times in my own life.

The most glaring example of a time I made this mistake happened early in my ministry. When Denise and I first got married, we worked together in a denominational church. It was a wonderful church, and we served under a godly, seasoned pastor. We enjoyed our years of ministry there, but it was also an intense learning period for me — a season when areas of spiritual immaturity at times were exposed so I could deal with them.

Certainly one of these times occurred when I became offended by something the pastor did and then allowed that offense to become a big issue in my mind. As a result, when the Lord spoke to my heart and said, *"Your time here is finished. I want you to leave this church,"* my mind wanted to add my own natural thoughts and opinions to that instruction. The offense I had allowed to fester wanted to crowd in and influence the internal discussion!

I thought, *Okay, I'm to leave, but then what? What am I supposed to do next?* I didn't receive an answer to my question at that time — but if I'd just taken that first step of obedience, God would have given me the next step. Instead, I made the same mistake Abraham and the apostle Paul made. God said something; then I tried to figure out the rest of His plan on my own.

I decided to get alone with my own thoughts by renting a room in a hotel in town for a couple of days. This way I could think about what we were to do next. The problem was that I was getting alone more with my own thoughts fueled by offense than I was seeking to know what the Lord was saying to me.

During my time in that hotel, I had this thought: *The people of this city need a pastor who really loves them. It's time for you to start your own church in this city.* Added to that thought was the fact that Denise and I loved the city we were in. We already had a house there, and we had friends and contacts in the city. Putting together the facts as I saw them — with my perspective skewed by the offense I had yet to repent of — I *assumed* it was the will of God for us to start a church in that city. It just "seemed" to make sense.

But what *seems* to make sense isn't always right. Remember what Proverbs 16:25 (*NKJV*) says: "There is a way that seems right to a man, but its end is the way of death."

So under my misguided thinking, Denise and I started a church that was never the plan of God — and do you know what happened? If you guessed that *nothing* happened, you'd be right!

For two years we struggled, and there was minimal fruit to be seen from our efforts. I was embarrassed to even show my face in public because our church was so tiny. The church we had come from was huge and successful — quite a contrast to the one we had started. It was a tiny work that didn't seem to have any blessing on it at all.

On top of that, Denise and I were oppressed in our souls. Our minds, will, and emotions were worn to a frazzle, and we were spiritually depleted of energy and hope. If that wasn't enough, our bank accounts were also on empty,

> What *seems* to make sense isn't always right. Remember what Proverbs 16:25 (*NKJV*) says: "There is a way that seems right to a man, but its end is the way of death."

leaving us unable to pay the staff's salaries and often even unable to buy groceries for our small family.

I'll never forget one particularly bad week. I ran out of gas five times because we didn't have any money. It's pretty bad when you pull up to a gas station and can only buy 25 cents' worth of gas! That's the desperate conditions Denise and I were living in.

Miserable is the best word I can use to describe our quality of life. We spent two years trying to breathe life into something God had not called us to do. It was one of the most miserable experiences of my life.

Yes, there were some people who were touched, which was an act of God's mercy. But we were in the wrong place, doing the wrong thing. Ironically, almost everyone else could see that we were out of the will of God — everyone, that is, except me.

> We spent two years trying to breathe life into something God had not called us to do. It was one of the most miserable experiences of my life.

I just kept thinking, *We're going to get a breakthrough! We're going to get a break-through!* But no matter how hard we tried, we couldn't make it happen. It didn't matter how much I prayed in the Spirit, exercised my faith, or tried to walk in love with others, nothing changed. Denise and I had no joy, no victory, and no money.

Finally, God in His mercy spoke to me one day and said, *"Rick, the church you have started is an Ishmael. It is not the promised Isaac that I wanted you to have. This is something you've done by yourself in your own strength. You only partially obeyed Me. Yes, I told you to leave the church you were at, but I did not tell you to start this one."*

That was a difficult word from the Lord for me to hear, but He was so right. We had only partially obeyed God, and as a result, we were in the wrong place and doing the wrong thing. He had told us to leave the denominational church where we were working, but everything else we had done from that point on was my own concoction based on false assumptions.

The truth is, you and I can think we hear God say anything we *want* to hear. Our emotions can often be so strongly attached to something that they masquerade as the voice of God. Therefore, we must be careful to *know that we know* we are hearing from Him and that what we believe He is saying is confirmed in the mouth of two or three reliable witnesses (*see* 2 Corinthians 13:1).

I made the same mistake that Abraham made. It's the same mistake many great leaders of the Bible — and possibly even you — have made.

God told me to leave the church, nothing more. But because there was no immediate additional direction, I added my own misguided interpretation to what He said. If I had obeyed the first simple mandate and then waited for God to give me the next step we were to take, He would have faithfully done so. But when I added my own step according to my natural reasoning, I introduced confusion into the equation and caused a delay in God's preplanned adventure for our lives.

> The truth is, you and I can think we hear God say anything we want to hear. Our emotions can often be so strongly attached to something that they masquerade as the voice of God.

After two years of pushing to make something happen, I was finally able to say that I was wrong. The truth is, I was quite stubborn and proud, and I really wanted the church to work. I had known in my heart for quite some time that I had made a mistake in starting the church, but I hadn't been willing to admit it.

Admitting I was wrong was quite humiliating. From the beginning, I had announced our glorious plans of building a great ministry and helping to bring revival to that city. But all my plans were fortified only by self-effort. In the end, I had to humble myself, stand before the people, and say, "I'm sorry, guys, I missed it. I thought I had heard from God, but I didn't."

> **All God wanted me to do was to faithfully take the first step, and then He would show me the next one. He didn't want me to lean on my own understanding and try to figure out my next move myself.**

The little church that Denise and I pastored was a failure. But here's the good news: Failure is a great place for success to begin! I had gotten off track, but I was ready and willing to get back *on* track. All God wanted me to do was to faithfully take the first step, and then He would show me the next one. He didn't want me to lean on my own understanding and try to figure out my next move myself. He wanted me to trust in Him with all my heart and acknowledge Him in all my ways. As I stayed faithful to do that, He would be faithful to direct my path.

And the same holds true for you.

HAS GOD GIVEN *YOU* DIRECTION?

God has a good plan for your life! He says, "'For I know the plans I have for you,' says the Lord. 'They are plans for good and not for disaster, to give you a future and a hope'" (Jeremiah 29:11 *NLT*). Your mind may not easily grasp or comprehend God's plan, but He will make it clear to you, just as He did for Abram. Even if your mind says, *Tilt, tilt, tilt! I don't understand this,* you will know in your heart when God speaks to you. If you will carefully and obediently follow His instructions, you will experience His blessings.

You may be in the same position as Abram or the apostle Paul or me. Perhaps God has told you to do something challenging or contrary to your natural way of thinking. He might have told you to start a business or go into ministry, to give a large amount of money to a worthy organization, or to believe for something that seems impossible to attain. Whatever instruction He may have given, you know that He has spoken to you, and He has even confirmed what He said. In fact, He has been dealing with you about it almost every day — but in your mind, you just can't seem to make sense of it.

You wonder, *Could this really be what God wants? It just doesn't make sense.* And because you haven't fully grasped His initial instructions, you have only partially followed the direction He has given you. As a result, you are living in a place of stagnation, with no ongoing experience of true joy or victory.

You may have even blamed your situation on the devil. But it's important to face this reality: If you haven't taken action on *all* that God told you to do, your lack of full obedience can actually provide a foothold for the enemy in your life that he wouldn't otherwise have.

Has God told you to do something, but you haven't done it yet? Or have you only done *part* of what He has asked? If you were honest with yourself, would you have to admit that you've added your own interpretation to what He has said to you? If your answer is yes to any of these questions, you need to face the reality that you have set yourself up to experience unnecessary problems in life.

Partial obedience is fertile ground for producing a life of struggle, frustration, financial lack, broken relationships, and a host of other problems. But the good news is, you can change your course! If you're in this situation, you can be assured that the Holy Spirit is tugging on your heart right now, telling you, *"This is not My plan for your life. You have taken a detour. Let Me help you make adjustments so you can get fully in My will for you. When you do, things will change."*

> If you haven't taken action on *all* that God told you to do, your lack of full obedience can actually provide a foothold for the enemy in your life that he wouldn't otherwise have.

Yes, the distance from where you are to where God wants you to be may seem huge. It may seem difficult for you to take this step of faith. But could it be any more difficult than what you're experiencing right now? The truth is, you will not be happy or successful until you're *fully obedient* to God's will. Although challenges will come, every part of your life will begin to flourish the way it was always meant to when you are right in the middle of God's will for you.

So why not take that step today? Determine to immerse yourself fully in the will of God. If you've been partially obedient or you've taken a detour of your own making, ask Him to forgive you and to give you the strength to completely obey what He has asked you to do.

When you fully align yourself with what you *know* is God's will for you, things *will* get better. That doesn't mean you won't face opposition because you will. But the power and the favor of God will go with you wherever you go. Money, material possessions, and everything you need to fulfill His plan will come to you when you need it as you trust Him. As He promised in Psalm

84:11, "...No good thing will he withhold from them that walk uprightly."

So don't be wise in your own eyes. Fear the Lord, turning away from the evil of pride (*see* Proverbs 3:7). Seek the face of God, and quiet your heart to hear His voice. He has said that as you seek Him with all your heart, you *will* find Him. He has promised, "I will guide you along the best pathway for your life. I will advise you and watch over you" (Psalm 32:8 *NLT*). Simply trust Him to make good on His Word in your life as you do what He instructs you to do every step of the way.

> **The truth is, you will not be happy or successful until you're *fully obedient* to God's will.**

Think About It

1. As we've seen from the life of Abram, it doesn't pay to partially obey the commands of God. Partial obedience is actually disobedience, and it delays God's plan for your life.

   What specific direction do you know that God has given you for your life? Is your heart assured that you are engaged in doing everything He has asked you to do — the way He wants you to do it? If not, can you pinpoint what part of His instruction you may not have followed through on yet? What are you going to do about that area of disobedience going forward?

2. Ask yourself: *Have I added my own interpretation to what I know God has told me to do?* If the answer is possibly yes, get quiet before God and ask Him to show you how to make adjustments to get you back in His perfect will for your life.

3. Abram was on a journey that took him to the right place — Canaan — but he was with the wrong people. God had not told him to bring Lot, Nahor, Terah, or anyone else along with him besides his wife and his own servants and livestock.

   Are you in the right place but perhaps connected to the wrong people? What has God been prompting you to do about certain relationships in your life? Are you taking steps to fully obey Him in this area?

4. Jesus said that He is the Good Shepherd, you are His sheep, and you can hear His voice (*see* John 10:14,27). What has God spoken to your heart that you are still struggling to make sense of? Write it down, and then ask Him to clarify His instruction. Determine beforehand that once you understand what God has asked you to do, you will trust Him for the grace and the wisdom to do it *His* way.

CHAPTER SIX

IT MAY BE TIME TO REDIRECT AND GET FOCUSED!

I want to take the discussion further on one of the pitfalls to avoid that we talked about in the last chapter. As we seek to follow God's will in our lives, we must make sure that *when God reveals something about His will for our lives, we don't try to add to or change what He says to fit our own natural reasoning.*

In this chapter, I'll give you two more examples — one from the life of the apostle Paul, and one from my own life. Regarding my own journey of following after God's call, I'll take up where I left off in the last chapter — during that season in the early years of ministry that proved to be such an intense learning period for me.

As I said, after leaving the denominational church where Denise and I had served as associates, we started a church that was not part of God's plan for our lives. His will went in one direction, and Denise and I had gone in another direction — and He didn't adjust His plans and purposes to accommodate us! Once I came to my senses and the Lord showed me that we had birthed an "Ishmael," we decided to get back on track.

The first thing I had to do was resign my position, even though I didn't know what in the world we were going to do next. It was very scary, but we decided it was the right thing to do.

Once you realize you've made a mistake and have gone in a direction that isn't God's will for you, don't keep "beating that dead horse." If you're in the wrong place, just admit what's already obvious to God; then seek Him to find out how to get back on the path of *His* will for your life.

> If you're in the wrong place, just admit what's already obvious to God; then seek Him to find out how to get back on the path of *His* will for your life.

Two years had passed since God had originally told us to leave the denominational church where I had been an associate and from where I had taken a detour that led us off track. I'm grateful for all the lessons I learned during those two difficult years. I realize that God can use anything in our lives to teach us, even when we miss the mark and do things our own way. However, I'm also very aware of the difference it would have made if I had carefully obeyed God when He first spoke to me and had not veered from following His direction. We would have stayed right on track in God's perfect timing instead of having to trust Him to redeem the time we lost.

But as Denise and I stood in front of our little "Ishmael" church for the last time, we weren't sure what we were supposed to do next. We knew only that God wanted us to leave the city and state, so as a first step, we decided to move back to my hometown of Tulsa where my family lived.

It seemed as if every strike was against us, but a lack of money was the biggest problem we faced. We were so poor when it came time to leave Arkansas that we couldn't even pay for the gas in our car, not to mention the toll fees to enter the next town. We literally had no financial reserves to draw from for that trip.

We held a garage sale and tried to sell everything we could to generate some fast cash so we could pack up and move to Tulsa. Furniture, bedding, clothes, and kitchenware were all liquidated. We had been married only a few years, so we had many wedding gifts that we also put up for sale, keeping only a few of them for ourselves.

That garage sale brought in enough money to pay for gas and toll fees from Arkansas to Oklahoma — a trip of approximately 120 miles. It also enabled us to rent a very small U-Haul so we could pack it with our few possessions, hook it to the back of our car, and head west. We drove to my parents' Tulsa home and unloaded what was left of our belongings in their garage.

My dad asked me, "Son, what are you going to do?"

"I don't know, Dad," was the only reply I had to give him.

We really had no idea what our next steps were to be. But my parents were supportive and kind enough to let us stay in their home with them and regroup as we tried to figure out how to get back on track with God's will for our lives.

For the next 30 days, I wondered, *What ARE we going to do?* That's about how long it took for me to get quiet enough to hear what the Holy Spirit was saying to my heart as He revealed our next step. I couldn't hear Him when we were in Arkansas. We had to leave there and get in a new environment so my heart could get quiet and my mind could get clear enough to hear Him speak.

Finally, at the end of those 30 days, God's word of direction came: *We were to begin an itinerant teaching ministry.* This time I wasn't going to make a mistake. (Once you've made a mistake like the one we'd made, you don't want to miss it again!) I wrote down exactly what He said to me and didn't add one thing to it. In fact, I didn't even ask too many questions. I just said, "Yes, Lord. Whatever You say is what we'll do."

The moment we got in line with God's plan for us, divine favor showed up and His blessings began to pour into our lives. We were finally going the right direction, and we had learned a crucial lesson: *Knowing and being in the will of God is the key to success.* That's where blessing, favor, and power are found — right in the middle of God's will.

Doors began to open for our ministry, and things changed almost overnight. It was truly miraculous! Power, protection, and provision came, along with answers, favor, and incredible opportunities.

> The moment we got in line with God's plan for us, divine favor showed up and His blessings began to pour into our lives.

During our last two years in Arkansas, the world had seemed to settle into a dull, black-and-white existence. But once we arrived in Tulsa, it was like someone turned on the light and displayed a full spectrum of color. It was as if we had stepped out of a desert and into paradise. The gifts of God inside me that had been so constricted in Arkansas began to powerfully burst forth.

Of course, Arkansas is a beautiful state filled with lovely people. It just wasn't the right place for *me*.

It's all about the plan of God for a person's life. Every place is the right place for someone. If God is the One who plants a person in a certain place, that soil is fertile ground for that person to flourish as he obeys what God has called him to do.

But for me, my gift to teach had been obscured in the surroundings where we'd situated ourselves in the past season. Now that gift was finally on the road where it was supposed to be — ministering to congregations from the Word of God, setting lives free, and digging deep to pull out nuggets of truth that the people I was ministering to needed to hear or had never seen or heard before. We had gotten back on track and were in the right environment — the one God had planned for us that was more conducive to the development of our gifts and calling.

> Every place is the right place for someone. If God is the One who plants a person in a certain place, that soil is fertile ground for that person to flourish as he obeys what God has called him to do.

What Denise and I learned through this experience was critical. When we are in God's will, we may still encounter struggles and challenges along the way. But supernatural favor and blessing will operate in our lives, regardless of resistance.

ATHENS: PAUL'S BIG STEP IN THE RIGHT DIRECTION

As we have established throughout the past few chapters, Paul heard the prophetic order of God's will clearly described for his life. Yet by all appearances, it seems apparent that it was a process for Paul to come to a place of full focus on that exact order in his ministry. A study of Paul's actions and experiences in the first several years of his ministry also leads one to reasonably conclude that as a result, he met with unnecessary resistance.

Jesus Himself had instructed Paul to bring the Gospel *first* to the Gentiles, then to kings and governments, and *lastly* to the children of Israel (*see* Acts 9:15). But for a number of reasons, including an overwhelming burden to see his fellow Hebrews saved, Paul kept going to the Jews in each new city he entered as a matter of first priority.

We've seen that in the first years of Paul's apostolic ministry, he repeated this pattern of ministry in every city he entered. That included the city of Berea. There Paul initially found favor with some of the Jewish listeners as he shared the Gospel message. But the atmosphere quickly deteriorated when hostile Jews from Thessalonica, the last city where Paul had ministered, came to stir up trouble for his ministry (*see* Acts 17:10-13). As a result, Paul once again fled for his life and traveled to the city of Athens alone. But his arrival in Athens proved to be a major milestone in his ministry.

PAUL ON HIS OWN — A STRATEGIC POSITIONING

There Paul was, walking through Athens with no traveling companions, which was very unusual for Paul. Silas and Timothy had helped him safely depart from Berea during the night, but had remained in Berea (*see* Acts 17:14). Barnabas had parted company with him much earlier when they sharply disagreed about whether or not to take John Mark on the second missionary journey (*see* Acts 15:37-40). For the first time ever recorded, Paul was alone on an apostolic journey, and this landmark moment occurred in the city of Athens — one of the most zealously pagan Gentile cities in the Roman Empire at that time.

A person couldn't have entered a more Gentile environment in New Testament times than Athens. It was the ancient religious capital of the pagan world, once the zenith of idolatry.

This was definitely not a place Paul would have desired to go by himself. In fact, the apostle immediately sent word back to Timothy and Silas through those who had brought him to Athens, saying in essence, "Please get here as quickly as you can. I don't want to spend too much time here alone" (*see* Acts 17:15). However, it would be quite awhile before Paul's companions joined him. By then, the apostle had left Athens and traveled on to Corinth.

Naturally speaking, Paul wasn't drawn to Gentiles, much less to those in such a pervasively pagan city such as Athens. He was a Hebrew of Hebrews, a Pharisee of Pharisees, and a Jew through and through. He had been raised so differently from the people whom God had put at the top of his priority list in ministry. And although he had almost inadvertently reached a limited number of Gentiles along the way, Paul had yet to really focus his attention on them.

It is therefore very significant that Paul was alone in Athens. Sometimes a person has to be by himself so he can really hear and understand the will of God, and that was Paul's situation at this point in his ministry. He didn't choose to go to Athens alone, but as a result of the way circumstances transpired, that was the outcome. And it was in Athens, in this moment of aloneness, that Paul came face to face with the foremost call for his life. It was there that he immersed himself in the Gentile

> Sometimes a person has to be by himself so he can really hear and understand the will of God, and that was Paul's situation at this point in his ministry.

world. Because he was alone, he couldn't talk to Silas, Timothy, or Barnabas about it. In Athens, it was just Paul and God.

WHAT WAS ATHENS *REALLY* LIKE?

When Paul arrived in Athens, he walked approximately five miles along a road lined with thousands of idols. As the apostle walked to the center of the town, "…he saw [that] the city wholly given to idolatry" (Acts 17:16). Along the way, he passed the famous cemetery of Athens. This cemetery featured idols and statues of all kinds and the graves of some of the greatest idolaters in human history, including many well-known pagan philosophers and politicians. There were so many "gods" in this city that one Roman satirist of the First Century wrote that it was "easier to find a god than to find a man" in Athens.[1]

As Paul continued on his journey into the heart of the city, he encountered more idols positioned on pedestals — some of them dressed and some of them naked. They were primarily crafted from white marble but had been painted to look lifelike. Skin had been painted to look like real flesh; hair was painted to look like real hair; and the eyes were marbleized so that when passersby looked at these idols, the eyes glistened as if the gods were looking back at them.

At the end of the road, Paul came to the marketplace. The word "market" is a translation of the Greek word *agora*, which is the old Greek word describing *the place of commerce, trade, slave-trading, and debate.* It, too, was a place filled with idolatry. Hundreds of statues stood on pedestals surrounding the marketplace. A number of pagan temples adjoined the agora, indicating just how central idolatry was to the lives of the Athenians. When

---

[1]Lyman Abbott, *The Life and Letters of the Apostle Paul* (Boston, MA: Houghton, Mifflin & Company, 1898), p. 46.

people came to buy their goods, they often went into the temple as well to worship the gods and offer sacrifices to them. All of this and more is what the apostle Paul experienced as he made his way through the city of Athens for the first time.

PAUL SURVEYS THE CITY

Once Paul sent word for Timothy and Silas to join him, he "...waited for them at Athens, [and] his spirit was stirred in him, when he saw the city wholly given to idolatry" (Acts 17:16). Paul must have felt like a solitary island in a toxic sea that was churning and foaming with paganism.

As a newcomer, Paul surely climbed the steps of the great Acropolis and surveyed the city. The Acropolis represented the very height of worldwide paganism. It stood on top of the mountain overlooking the city and had a complex of buildings, including the Parthenon where the great statue of the goddess Athena stood. From the top of this mountain, Paul would have had a perfect vantage point to observe this Gentile populace — the very type of people to whom Jesus had originally called him — as they milled around the marketplace and the city's many temples.

> **Paul must have felt like a solitary island in a toxic sea that was churning and foaming with paganism.**

So Paul began ministering the Gospel in one of the most Gentile cities in the world. Although he did spend a relatively brief period of time reasoning with the Athenian Jews in their synagogue (*see* Acts 17:17), his kinsmen were not his focus in this city. This time Paul made his way daily to Athens' agora, preaching the Gospel message to a crowd that was far from God and His promises. These were people immersed in pagan occultism, perverse sex, and intellectualism — in spiritual darkness and without hope. But they were precisely the people to whom Paul had been called, and in Athens, he found himself standing in the midst of them — all alone.

PAUL SPEAKS TO THE GREEKS ON MARS HILL

Although the market was a place of commerce, like all of Athens, it was also a spiritually dark, oppressive place. It was filled with and surrounded by explicit statues depicting the Greek gods. On any given day, people would be shopping for their food going and coming back from one of the temples in the neighborhood. Others would be walking to the public baths for an afternoon of relaxation and sexual perversion, which was considered the norm to them. Philosophers and debaters would gather at one central location in the market to listen and argue about their beliefs and points of view. Slave traders sold and bought slaves right next to those who traded and sold livestock.

This was the "market" where Paul preached in Athens. It was *not* the perfect atmosphere for preaching by any stretch of the imagination. But when a minister is pioneering a work or working in a territory where no one has gone before him, he sometimes has to take advantage of whatever opportunity is available to him. As Paul surveyed the city, it must have become apparent to him that the market was the best place for him to reach the people of the city — so he made the most of the opportunity!

One day the apostle Paul ascended the stone steps to the public podium in the section of the market where people assembled together to listen to philosophers and debaters who came to draw a crowd and share their ideas. Thus began Paul's ministry in that city of reasoning daily with those who gathered to listen in the debaters' section of Athens' market.

Acts 17:18 goes on to tell us, "And certain philosophers of the Epicureans, and of the Stoics, encountered him. And some said, What will this babbler say? Others said, He seemeth to be a setter forth of strange gods: because he preached unto them Jesus, and the resurrection."

These Greek philosophers and intellectuals called Paul a "babbler," which comes from the Greek word *spermologos*. This word is a compound of the words *sperm*, the Greek word for *seed*, and the word *logos*, the Greek word for *words*. But when compounded as they are in this text, the new word depicts *a person who seeds a crowd with words, thoughts, or ideas*. This means these Epicureans and Stoics were asking, "Who is this person who is seeding us with words, thoughts, and ideas that we've never heard before?"

These Greek philosophers didn't realize how right they were when they called Paul a "babbler"! Every day he stood in the market preaching and thereby habitually seeding that crowd with the heart-piercing truth of God's Word. The apostle stood at that public podium like a farmer, throwing his "seed-words" into the ground of the people's hearts. Some of the hearts of those who listened proved to be good ground that would receive those seeds and produce a harvest.

Paul knew what Jesus taught during His earthly ministry — that some hearts are stony, some are shallow, and some are good ground that will produce a 30-, 60-, or 100-fold return. Regardless, Paul preached on, believing that some of the Word he was preaching was falling on ground that would eventually produce a harvest for the Kingdom of God.

As a result of Paul's perpetual persistence, he eventually got the Athenians' attention! He seeded that crowd so regularly, so consistently, and with such great effect that Acts 17:19 says, "And they took him, and brought him unto *Areopagus*, saying, May we know what this new doctrine, whereof thou speakest, is?" (Acts 17:19).

The Areopagus was the most prestigious place in the entire nation to share a new idea. It was the place where the judges and intelligentsia of the city came together to exchange, discuss, and debate the latest concepts. If anyone had something new to say, the person would often be brought to the Areopagus to present it.

The Areopagus was also a criminal court that at times was used, as in this verse, to determine whether or not new doctrines were considered legal. There was no higher court in Athens, and for Paul to be summoned to this court meant that he finally had gotten the attention of the city with his "daily" preaching in the market. The most brilliant and respected minds in all of ancient Greece wanted to hear Paul's message for themselves in the highest court of Athens.

So these learned men of Athens brought Paul to this honored forum, and as the apostle stood in the midst of this intellectual crowd, they gave him the opportunity to explain the Gospel to all who were assembled. Paul's message in this setting is recorded in Acts 17:22-31. Acts 17:20 tells us that those in attendance said, "...Thou bringest us certain strange things to our ears: we would know therefore what these things mean."

Notice these Gentiles said, "For thou bringest us certain *strange things*...." The words "strange things" are from a Greek word that conveys *something that is startling, shocking, surprising, strange, or scandalous*. Paul's message of Jesus, the Cross, and the Resurrection was so far out of the range of normality for these Athenians that they found it to be completely *scandalous*. To hear that God died on the Cross for mankind and shed His own blood for redemption — that was a *startling* message to their ears!

All around the apostle stood an audience of the brightest, most intellectual, and most sophisticated minds in Greece at that time. This was a huge open door for Paul. These judges of the land were asking him to fully explain his message. As members of the highest court of the land, these men were poised to listen. Then afterward they would be required to pass judgment on Paul's ideas that were so strange to their Greek way of thinking and to render a legal decision regarding him and his message.

As Paul began to preach to these educated people, every word had to be carefully chosen and spoken under the anointing of the Holy Spirit. There was no room for error in his words on that day.

Paul didn't scold the audience for being idolaters. He didn't rebuke them for their perversions. He didn't lecture them about their morals. He didn't even tell them they were wrong. If he had done any of these things, he would have immediately lost his entire audience — they would have tuned him out or left altogether.

Instead, Paul operated with strategic wisdom *by using something from the Greeks' own culture to reach them.* Earlier when he had walked through the city, the apostle had found an altar erected to "the Unknown God" (*see* Acts 17:23). When Paul saw that, a thought from Heaven must have lodged in his heart: *Here's a tool I can use to preach in Athens!* And when the time came to preach a key sermon to this Gentile audience, Paul employed that tool!

But Paul didn't just utilize that pagan altar as an illustration — he also quoted a famous Greek poet as he explained the Gospel. He wisely packaged his message using literature that was close to the hearts of his audience.

In all of these ways, Paul employed a brilliant strategy when speaking to his Gentile listeners. However, there was one crucial element lacking in the apostle's preaching to the intelligentsia of

Athens. Although Paul was excellent in his intellectual approach, there is no record of any demonstration of the Holy Spirit's supernatural power in Athens — no indication that the gifts of the Spirit were in operation there or that any signs and wonders attested to the truth of Paul's message.

When Paul concluded his message in the Athenian court, he had a very mixed response to his sermon. Acts 17:32,33 tells us, "And when they heard of the resurrection of the dead, some mocked: and others said, We will hear thee again of this matter. So Paul departed from among them."

Verse 32 tells us that "some mocked" when they heard Paul's message. The word "mocked" is derived from the Greek word *echidna*, which is the word for *a poisonous viper*. By using this vivid word, the Holy Spirit lets us know that when Paul concluded his masterful message, one group was so furious because of what Paul preached that they wanted to "get their fangs into him"!

> There was one crucial element lacking in the apostle's preaching to the Athenian intelligentsia. Although Paul was excellent in his intellectual approach, there is no indication that the gifts of the Spirit were in operation there or that any signs and wonders attested to the truth of Paul's message.

But there were other reactions to Paul's message as well. Acts 17:32 goes on to tell us, "...Others said, We will hear thee again of this matter." This second group wasn't jumping and shouting, "Amen!" But the fact that they were open-minded and wanted to hear Paul again constituted a significant victory for the Kingdom of God. This means they were interested — and for judges in the highest court of this pagan land to be interested in the Gospel was a huge development. *They wanted to hear more*, and that let Paul know that he still had an open door into their hearts.

Acts 17:33 says, "So Paul departed from among them." The Bible doesn't explicitly say how Paul felt when he walked out of the court. However, we do know that he had enraged one group, interested another group, and had no visible proof that anyone would be saved as a result of his preaching that day. It is likely that he felt like a failure or thought he hadn't ministered as powerfully as he had hoped.

Some Athenians did repent, including Dionysius the Areopagite, a woman named Damaris, and a few others (v. 34). However, for the most part, Paul's efforts in Athens produced minimal fruit. Even so, the apostle's time in this city proved to be a pivotal moment in his life. It was during his stay in Athens that Paul finally began warming up to the idea of God's grace empowering him to reach into a Gentile audience.

Approximately five years had passed since the day Paul was launched by the Holy Spirit into his calling from the church in Antioch. He had traveled to many cities and preached the Gospel to many people. Certainly some were saved along the way; however, the overall effectiveness of this early ministry was relatively minimal. Who wants to go on a five-year mission trip and have just a little fruit to talk about? It is probably safe to surmise that it wasn't what Paul or anyone else expected.

But in Athens, Paul was finally positioned in the right place to minister to the right people — the Gentiles — according to his divine assignment. After he was finished in Athens, he departed and made his way toward the city of Corinth.

'AFTER THESE THINGS'

Acts 18:1 tells us, *"After these things* Paul departed from Athens, and came to Corinth."

The phrase "these things" could refer to what Paul had just previously experienced in Athens. It could also refer to *all* that had transpired in the apostle's ministry before that moment. This would include the struggles he had experienced over the previous five years — the seeming lack of success, minimal results, and what appeared as an unrelenting series of calamities that most often originated as a result of hostile Jews.

Although there was a significant amount of peripheral fruit among Gentiles who were attracted to Paul and his message during those early years, an honest assessment of that period of time reveals a pattern that can't be ignored. Paul had been run out of city after city, had been beaten numerous times, and had even spent time in jail. He had been stoned and left for dead; he had gotten some of his friends in trouble; and he had made Jews angry almost everywhere he went.

If Paul had published a report of his ministry, I'm not sure many people would have wanted to volunteer to go on a mission trip with him or to support his work! He didn't have a lot of wonderful testimonies of a thriving ministry to share. Instead, it seemed that in those earlier years, what Paul had was a track record of trouble everywhere he went.

One could argue, of course, that Paul's minimal fruit and the huge resistance he experienced was due to the fact that he was blazing a Gospel trail where few, if any, had gone before. But the outcomes of his ministry *after* those early years compared to how Paul *began* his ministry were markedly different, as we will see.

Paul left the city of Athens and began to make his way to Corinth — an approximate 50-mile trip over rugged terrain and rolling hills. Some speculate that he may have sailed there from the port in Athens to the port of Cenchrea, which was near Corinth. This is possible, but most scholars generally agree that he walked the road to Corinth.

Since he was still traveling alone, the apostle had a lot of time to think. During this 50-mile solo journey, Paul evidently took an honest inventory of those first five years of ministry, coming to a conclusion that marked a pivotal point in his life.

It's true that when you're alone, it provides time to be honest with yourself and with God. Time alone can be very healthy. You would do well to take a moment to consider that thought as it pertains to your own walk with God in this present season. Time alone with the Lord may be what you need right now. It helps you evaluate honestly what He has called you to do in this life. If necessary, you can seek Him for wisdom on making necessary course corrections. And if He reassures you that you're on track with your present direction, you can get clarity on the actions He wants you to take to *stay* on track as you move forward.

> Time alone with the Lord may be what you need right now. It helps you evaluate honestly what He has called you to do in this life.

As Paul contemplated and evaluated the fruit of his ministry, he must have wondered, *What is going to meet me when I arrive in Corinth? I don't want things to continue as they have been. Something has to change.* We can surmise this was the apostle's train of thought because he seems to have made some monumental decisions about his life and ministry — about things he would and would never do again — by the time he arrived in Corinth.

In fact, those 50 miles of walking to Corinth alone with God would become a real defining moment for the apostle Paul. Decisions were made that would dramatically impact the rest of his life and ministry.

When a person has gone through a series of bad experiences, that person usually reaches a stage at which he is ready to change and embrace whatever steps are needed to get on a new track. He or she doesn't want to keep repeating the same patterns of thought and action that have produced disappointment in the past.

Can you think of instances in your own life in which you made a series of mistakes in a particular area — until you finally came to the point of resolving that you would *not* continue making those same mistakes? Paul was apparently in that state of mind as he walked the distance between Athens and Corinth. He was ready to do whatever was needed to experience a greater level of the demonstration of God's power in his life and ministry. And by the time he arrived in Corinth, he had come to a conclusion that would forever alter the focus of his ministry.

How Did Corinth Compare to Athens?

In terms of paganism, going from Athens to the city of Corinth was like going from bad to worse. Whereas Athens was a thriving educational center of learning, Corinth represented "life in the gutter." Athens was a city of rampant idolatry, but it was "refined" idolatry lived out brilliantly by educated people. Corinth, on the other hand, was as low as low could get — a city world-famous for its sinfulness and founded on pagan practices and sexual perversion of all sorts. It was so renowned for this that even the pagans of Rome and other parts of the world used the nickname "Corinthian" to describe any person who lived a life of drunkenness and debauchery.

Corinth sat on an isthmus between northern and southern Greece, so a person traveling in that area would have to go through Corinth, whether he wanted to go east to west, west to east, south to north, or north to south. The city had two harbors — one that led straight to the Roman province of Asia and another to Italy. Great numbers of travelers and sailors entered in and out of Corinth's ports on a frequent basis, coming from all over the world to enjoy the city's pleasures of sex, sensuality, and an abundance of alcohol.

Corinth was certainly not a place where Paul would naturally have chosen to be. He knew of its wicked reputation and would have avoided the city at all costs if it had only been a matter of his personal preference. Remember, he had been raised a Pharisee, and as touching the Law, he was blameless (*see* Philippians 3:4-6). So for Paul to go to the city of Corinth required a major step of faith and obedience.

PAUL'S NEW BEGINNING IN CORINTH

Corinth had its fair share of temples to pagan gods, including those to Apollo and Zeus, as well as a significant and historical one dedicated to the worship of Aphrodite. Aphrodite was the goddess of sex, and the Greeks in Corinth believed a multitude of various kinds of blessings came from her. A tenet of their pagan religion was that a person was required to offer sacrifices to the goddess Aphrodite in order to enjoy prosperity in his life.

At one point in Corinth's history, there were as many as 1,000 prostitutes who served the worshipers of Aphrodite,[2] and citizens were encouraged to indulge in sexual relations with temple prostitutes to bring prosperity and blessing into their lives. The entire city was filled with immoral pagan practices — a world away from

---

[2]Strabo, *Geography*, VIII.6.20

the lifestyle and moral structure that Paul had grown up with and had been accustomed to all his life.

In First Corinthians 2:3, we find a clue regarding what Paul was thinking and feeling as he walked from Athens to Corinth. Evidently he made some crucial decisions along the way that would define his ministry from that point forward. In that verse, Paul wrote to the Corinthian believers and recalled his early ministry to them, saying, "And I was with you in weakness, and in fear, and in much trembling."

This verse indicates that Paul had made the unalterable decision at that point in his life to focus on his primary call and not to be deterred from it. Knowing that he had made this commitment, he also knew there was no turning back. This was the backdrop to Paul's words in verse 3: "I was with you in weakness, and in fear, and in much trembling." The word "with" is the Greek word *pros*, which means *to be face to face*. A better translation of verse 3 would be, "*And when I saw your faces and was with you face to face, I was with you in much weakness, much fear, and in much trembling.*"

> The easiest place to make a decision is when you're in your prayer closet all by yourself. The real test of how seriously you take your own decision will be revealed when you come out of the place of prayer and have to face reality.

Paul's experience is a lesson to glean from in your own walk with the Lord. You need to understand that the easiest place to make a decision is when you're in your prayer closet all by yourself. The real test of how seriously you take your own decision will be revealed when you come out of the place of prayer and have to face reality.

For example, perhaps you have been alone in prayer and you've made this statement multiple times in your life: "I'm going start eating correctly, lose weight, and begin an exercise program!" When it was just you spending time with the Lord, it was easy for you to make that decision. But then you came out of your prayer time and were faced with the temptation of foods you don't need. Or the treadmill was shouting at you from the corner that it was time to exercise. These are the crucial moments that reveal the truth about how serious you were about the commitment you made in your conversation with God.

This is a common challenge for all of us to overcome in our spiritual walk. It's amazing how easy it is to conveniently forget what we decided to change when we were before the Lord in prayer and His Spirit was speaking to our hearts.

In First Corinthians 2:4, Paul wrote, "And my speech and my preaching was not with enticing words of man's wisdom, but in demonstration of the Spirit and of power."

It is my belief that this verse reveals Paul's struggles to come to grips with his divine call to focus on Gentiles — a people he didn't feel naturally comfortable with. It seems that his solitary experience in Athens was a time of "warming up" to a fuller understanding of his call to preach to the Gentiles. Then came the 50-mile walk to Corinth, during which there was much time alone for Paul to ponder the events and the fruit produced during his apostolic ministry up to that moment. And at some point as he walked to Corinth, the apostle made a decision from which he would not retreat, as we can surmise from his words in First Corinthians 2:3-5.

> It's amazing how easy it is to conveniently forget what we decided to change when we were before the Lord in prayer and His Spirit was speaking to our hearts.

Paul's arrival in Corinth marked the dawn of a new day and a new way of doing ministry. Although he originally went to the synagogue in Corinth, it wasn't long until he redirected his energies to the Gentiles. At long last, he was putting his primary focus on the prophetic order that God had designed for his life. Paul had realigned himself with God's plan that was given to him when he first came to Christ.

Paul's words in First Corinthians 2:4 tell us that the results of that decision he made were simply astounding. Signs, wonders, and mighty deeds followed Paul as he preached the Word to the Corinthian pagans, demonstrating the truth of his message. Paul found remarkable favor with multitudes of Gentiles who responded positively to his message — and as a result, he established a large, powerful church in the city of Corinth.

Do You Need To Make a Course Adjustment?

We've seen that Paul's first mighty results in ministry occurred after he redirected his focus to preach to the Gentiles as a matter of top priority.

It is clear that Paul believed the Jew had the right to hear the Gospel first (*see* Acts 13:46). The apostle demonstrated this again and again in the way he attempted to quickly reach Jewish communities when he first entered a city. Paul even stated from Romans 1:16 that the Gospel was to the Jew first.

However, it was proven time and time again that Paul rarely found receptivity with Jews in his own ministry. They generally didn't want to hear his message, and they caused the majority of his problems. But when the apostle eventually turned his attention more fully to his primary calling, he found himself graced with unusual favor and success. Although it was the apostle's custom to try to reach Jews first with the Gospel message, his divine call was first to the Gentiles — and as it turned out, they were the people whose hearts were generally more wide open and receptive to Paul's message.

Consider this lesson gleaned from the apostle Paul's life in light of your own walk with God. Are you focusing on the right path that God has ordained for your life?

Perhaps you need to tell your spouse, your family, your church, or your team members in your business, "Guys, we're going to make a course adjustment." It may be a humbling experience to admit that you've focused on the wrong thing. But once you do, you will be able to focus on setting your life in divine order — and as a result, favor will abound and blessings will overflow in your life.

Hold fast to what Jeremiah told us: "It is because of the Lord's mercy and loving-kindness that we are not consumed, because His [tender] compassions fail not. They are new every morning…" (Lamentations 3:22,23 *AMPC*). Realize that the Lord is on your side and wants to show you His tender mercies to get you where you need to be. I encourage you to open your heart and receive His compassion and the loving guidance of His Spirit right now. He will enable and empower you to *put your focus where it needs to be*!

Think About It

1. Have you gotten off track concerning something God told you to do? One way to help you know the answer to that question is to look at the fruit you are producing in your life. Do you have provision, protection, favor, peace, and joy for your journey — or are you suffering lack in these different areas of life? The lack of these things is not always a sign that you've gotten off track, but it often is an indicator that some area of your life needs your attention. I urge you to get quiet before the Lord in prayer and ask Him to reveal to you the truth.

2. Like the apostle Paul, do you find yourself somewhat alone in an unfamiliar place, possibly wondering why you are there? It may be that God is trying to speak to you, and the only way you can hear what He has to say is to be where you are. What adjustments can you make in your life to allow for more focused time in the Word and in prayer? As you take that extra time to seek the Lord, ask Him to give you ears to hear what His Spirit is speaking to your heart.

3. If you find that you are not walking fully in the will of God, what actions do you sense the Holy Spirit prompting you to take to get back on track? Do you need to go to someone and ask forgiveness for a past wrong? Is there something — an offense, a bad habit, a relationship — you need to let go of? Is there a step you can take toward fulfilling His plan that He has been asking you to take for a period of time? Perhaps it's time to reevaluate His instructions and to properly esteem even the smallest item on your list that He has given you to do.

CHAPTER SEVEN

ALIGNMENT WITH GOD'S WILL BRINGS BLESSING

*W*hen you align your life with God's plan for you, what happens is nothing short of miraculous. It doesn't mean you won't have challenges, because the devil will most certainly try to sidetrack you along the way. But if you'll stick with the plan of God and refuse to budge from it, He will release supernatural power and provision to help you.

We've seen that the apostle Paul's call was first and foremost to the Gentiles. In Romans 11:13, he even called himself the apostle to the Gentiles. Although Paul always had a plan to reach the Jews with the Gospel, a study of the apostle's ministry subsequent to Corinth reveals that the fruit of his ministry to Gentiles markedly increased after his time in that city, where he began focusing primarily on bringing the Gospel to the pagan population.

We've also seen that as a flagrantly pagan city, Corinth was not the place where Paul would have ever chosen to go in the natural. Nevertheless, it was where God wanted him at that time in his ministry. For Paul, Corinth was the right place, and the Gentile population of that city was the right people for him to center his attention on. As the apostle strategically realigned his focus on this divine priority for his life, it is apparent that he enjoyed an enormously successful period of ministry.

Instead of being chased out of town like so many times before, Paul was graced to stay for more than a year and a half — long enough to establish the Corinthian church. Several rough years of ministry had preceded this season, and there were still many intense challenges ahead. But Paul was finally operating in the prophetic order God had given him from the very outset of his ministry, and the results of that deliberate realignment would quickly become apparent to all as Paul experienced increased favor and blessing in his life.

Paul's story is a vivid demonstration of the central truth we're discussing — that knowing and being in the will of God is the key to success in this life. From that moment forward, it seems Paul more fully embraced his calling as an apostle to the Gentile world. It's true he also reached Jews as he traveled to new cities, as is clearly seen when he entered Ephesus (*see* Acts 18:19; 19:8,9). But a general overview of Paul's actions after Corinth makes it clear to me that his primary focus had shifted to the Gentile listeners. God's power literally erupted in Paul's life when he fully embraced the divine order for his ministry that was first given to him in Acts 9:15.

> God's power literally erupted in Paul's life when he fully embraced the divine order for his ministry that was first given to him in Acts 9:15.

DIVINE PROVISION

Let's look at one very important development that occurred as a result of Paul fine-tuning his alignment with God's will.

When Paul was first sent out from the Antioch church, there is no record that he received any financial help. In fact, there is no record of any financial support during the first several years of

Paul's apostolic ministry. These were the years when the apostle was focused primarily on reaching the Jews. During these early years, the goal of reaching Gentiles with the Gospel was still somewhat of an afterthought to him.

During that time period, Paul worked in the leatherworking trade he had learned as a young man in order to pay his bills so he wouldn't burden the churches he was serving (*see* 1 Corinthians 4:12; 9:6; 1 Thessalonians 2:9; 2 Thessalonians 3:8). The word for Paul's profession translated "tentmaker" is the Greek word *skeno-poios*, which referred to a wide range of activities, including the profession of making cloaks, curtains, shoes, or any products made from leather. Therefore, it's reasonable to conclude that although the manual profession Paul learned as a young man would have included tentmaking skills, it probably entailed much more.

It is likely that Paul worked in his trade at least occasionally in most cities he ministered in during those early years — Lystra, Iconium, Thessalonica, etc. — including when he first arrived in Corinth. But during the apostle's year and a half in Corinth, once he had at long last settled in to minister to the Gentiles, he apparently received a large offering of support that marked a shift in the financial provision for his ministry (*see* 2 Corinthians 11:9).

The offering came from the church at Philippi, and it was brought to Paul by Silas and Timothy when they traveled from Berea to Corinth to join him. At that time, Paul was already ministering to the Gentiles in Corinth.

To better understand the setting in which Paul received this supernatural offering, a deeper study of Acts 18:5 is necessary. This verse states that Paul was ministering to Jews and Gentiles in the synagogue in Corinth. But as soon as Silas and Timothy arrived, the *King James Version* says that Paul was "pressed in the spirit" to testify to the Jews.

Since Paul was already speaking to Jews in the synagogue — along with Gentiles who were present and hungry to learn — the *King James* wording seems to indicate that Paul was led by the Holy Spirit at that time to shift his focus primarily to the Jews and not to the Greeks. However, there is a serious problem with this translation. The oldest Greek texts emphatically do *not* say that Paul was "pressed in the spirit." In fact, the oldest manuscripts don't include the words "in the spirit" at all. The Greek in these older manuscripts can literally be read that Paul was *compelled* or *pressured* to direct his message to the Jews.

The inference is that when Timothy and Silas showed up, they were possibly surprised to see Paul putting so much of his attention on the Gentiles. Perhaps they didn't understand what he was doing and even pressured him back into his previous pattern of making Jews his first priority.

Scripture here is not entirely clear, but whatever the case, this compulsion that Paul felt clearly occurred concurrently with the arrival of Timothy and Silas. It seems Paul suddenly felt pressured to direct his ministry of the Word in a different direction. Were Timothy and Silas the source of that pressure? Possibly, since the original Greek text does *not* say it was something Paul sensed by the Spirit that he was to do. Whatever the source of the pressure, the Greek text is clear that the apostle only experienced this sense of compelling after Timothy and Silas joined him in Corinth.

However, Paul didn't give in to this pressure for long. It was only a short time after this that he determined, "That's it — I'm done with this! I'm going to the Gentiles" (*see* Acts 18:6).

It was against this backdrop of events that the offering from the church at Philippi was brought to Paul by Silas and Timothy when they traveled from Berea to Corinth to join him. According to Acts 18:5 and 6, Paul was pivoting his focus to the Gentiles at the time of their arrival. Right then financial resources suddenly showed up that enabled Paul to do the work of the ministry with less distraction. From that moment on, it seems the apostle was finally able to focus more on the preaching of the Word, to prayer, and to establishing the church in Corinth and wherever the Lord led in the years to come.

The longer you walk with God, the more you learn that He foots the bills when you are where He has asked you to be, doing what He has asked you to do. That doesn't mean you won't ever face financial challenges. But when you are doing what God has asked, your obedience opens the door to greater favor and provision.

However, it's important to understand that we cannot always measure success by finances. Sometimes when we are exactly where we're supposed to be and we're doing what God has asked us to do, the devil will try to resist us in the financial realm. That's when we have to *lay hold* of what we already know — that God is a faithful God whose promises are yes and amen (*see* 2 Corinthians 1:20)! Ultimately financial provision will come, along with favor and countless other blessings, when we get in agreement with God's will and hold fast to our trust in Him.

> The longer you walk with God, the more you learn that He foots the bills when you are where He has asked you to be, doing what He has asked you to do.

God knows what you have need of and will provide it according to His riches in glory when you intentionally take steps to line up with His revealed will for your life (*see* Philippians 4:19). Again, that doesn't mean you won't occasionally be financially challenged, because the devil is always at work in his attempts to distract you and get you to back off what God has asked you to do. But it's a spiritual

> **It's a spiritual law that deliberate and diligent obedience ultimately brings divine favor and blessings.**

law that deliberate and diligent obedience ultimately brings divine favor and blessings.

Isaiah 1:19 states, "If ye be willing and obedient, ye shall eat the good of the land." You'll see this law displayed again and again in your own walk with God as you align your life with what He has revealed to you about your time on this earth.

DIVINE POWER IS YOURS IN THE CENTER OF GOD'S WILL

The apostle Paul faced persecutions and obstacles that would have shattered any normal man. He listed in detail the hardships and hassles he encountered in Second Corinthians 11:23-27. He was beaten frequently, thrown in prison, stoned, shipwrecked three times, lost at sea, endangered by robbers and by fellow citizens, suffered hunger and thirst — and the list goes on and on.

What was it about Paul that caused him to rise up after every difficulty and challenge and keep moving forward? He possessed an unstoppable spirit and an indomitable determination to walk out God's revealed plan until he had fulfilled all that the Lord had given him to do.

There was one more very important ingredient that was in operation as Paul pursued his call — he continually embraced God's *grace*.

Grace is God's divine empowerment to do what we could never do on our own. It's His ability to live beyond our ability and carry out His will for our lives.

Whatever God is asking you to do, He will always provide whatever you need to do it. And where He guides you, He will also provide whatever it is you need to do the job. This is confirmed in Second Peter 1:3 (*NLT*):

> By his *divine power*, God has given us everything we need for living a godly life. We have received all of this by coming to know him, the one who called us to himself by means of his marvelous glory and excellence.

God's divine power is continually available to you and me by grace and in an exceedingly limitless supply (*see* Ephesians 2:7). It was with this in mind that Paul wrote: "And God is able to make *all grace* abound toward you, that you, always having all sufficiency in all things, may have an abundance for every good work" (2 Corinthians 9:8 *NKJV*).

Satan may try to stop you from doing the will of God, but never forget that he cannot prevail against you if you will yield to the Lord and stand fast on what He has told you to do. In those moments of intense opposition, you will find that God supplies you with more than enough grace to match whatever the enemy is trying to do. It's yours for the asking!

James 4:6 (*AMPC*) confirms this divine promise of grace, declaring, "But He gives us more and more grace (power of the Holy Spirit, to meet this evil tendency and all others fully). That is why He says, God sets Himself against the proud and haughty, but gives grace [continually] to the lowly (those who are humble enough to receive it)." So whenever your mind and emotions are being challenged to react to trying

> In those moments of intense opposition, you will find that God supplies you with more than enough grace to match whatever the enemy is trying to do. It's yours for the asking!

circumstances, pray and believe for God's Spirit to give you the grace and power you need in that exact moment (*see* Hebrews 4:16). God resists the proud, but He pours out empowering grace on behalf of those who are humble enough to receive it.

IS YOUR LIFE ALIGNED WITH GOD'S WILL?

So take a moment to ask yourself, *Is my life aligned with God's will, or am I doing my own will while pretending that it's God's?* Be honest with yourself: Does it seem like you are seldom happy or satisfied and often frustrated and exasperated — including frustrated financially? If your answer is yes, I want to encourage you to ask the Lord whether or not you're in the right place, doing the right thing. If you are in the will of God, it is likely that you're going to experience joy, peace, and fulfillment — even in the midst of hardships. But if your life is generally joyless and frustrating — if it seems like you go through one defeated experience after another — there's probably an adjustment that needs to take place in where you are or in what you're doing.

It's time to seek the Lord for His wisdom and direction. He will help you realign your life so His will can prosper in your life and you can enjoy a greater level of blessing than you have ever known in the past. I encourage you to let David's heart cry become *your* heart cry: "Teach me to do your will, for you are my God. May your gracious Spirit lead me forward on a firm footing" (Psalm 143:10 *NLT*).

And as you align your life with God's will, keep your heart wide open to receive His blessings. Those blessings are your spiritual birthright, and they include supernatural financial provision and every other good thing you need to accomplish His divine assignment for your life.

THINK ABOUT IT

1. What blessings have you experienced in your life as a result of obediently following God's will? How has He specifically provided for you financially? What does this say to you about God's character?

2. Have you ever gone through a time when you were *out* of the will of God? If so, consider how the Holy Spirit helped you realize that you were off track and then got you back on God's path for your life.

3. Once Paul fully aligned his life with God's will and began ministering to the Gentiles in the city of Corinth, countless numbers of people were saved. Consider this thought: There are those who might be unknowingly waiting on you to fully align your life with God's will so that they can be birthed into the Kingdom. How does the thought of other people needing you to help them secure Heaven as their eternal destination impact you? Does it motivate you to be fully obedient to God's call?

4. One of the priceless blessings of being in God's will is the open access to receive from His *grace*. What new aspects about God's divine power imparted through grace have you learned by reading this chapter? In what new ways are you motivated to draw upon His limitless supply of grace for the challenges you face in your daily life?

CHAPTER EIGHT

EXPECT DIVINELY DESIGNED APPOINTMENTS

*I*n order for us to effectively accomplish the will of God, we will need help. We cannot do on our own what we are called to do; we need the cooperation of other God-called members in the Body of Christ. Paul wrote about this truth to the Corinthian believers: "A spiritual gift is given to each of us so we can help each other.... The human body has many parts, but the many parts make up one whole body. So it is with the body of Christ.... And God has put each part just where he wants it" (1 Corinthians 12:7,12,18 *NLT*).

You will find that when you step out to obey what God has told you to do, He will put you together with the right people. He will supernaturally establish *divine connections* with other believers assigned to help you fully accomplish His will.

I found this to be true decades ago when the USSR was collapsing and God made it clear that He wanted Denise and me and our family to move to that region of the world to minister

> You will find that when you step out to obey what God has told you to do, He will supernaturally establish *divine connections* with other believers assigned to help you fully accomplish His will.

the Gospel. Today I see how very deliberate and strategic the Lord was when He told us to relocate to the former Soviet Union. The Lord was well aware of all the gifts and talents He had instilled in us that would be fruitful for His Kingdom in that part of the world.

To this day, I am still amazed to think of all the ways God orchestrated every event to move us across the planet and connect us with believers in that part of the world — specific individuals strategically called to work alongside us to carry out His amazing plan. Even before we arrived there, God was already miraculously moving on people's hearts to join us. We didn't know them and they didn't know us, but *He* knew all of us — and He knew exactly *who* needed to be at the same location *at the same time* so that we would supernaturally connect. God was at work, divinely assembling a team that would become a powerful tool for harvesting souls for His Kingdom.

God had given me a vision to teach the Bible to Soviet people, to launch churches, to start the first Christian television network, and to bring the teaching of the Bible to believers across the former Soviet Union. But something was missing. I had the call and the vision to start a great work for God's Kingdom in that part of the world. However, I didn't speak the language or understand the culture the way I needed to in order to fulfill the divine assignment. So at the same time God was preparing me and my family, He was also calling a small team to work alongside us in the implementation of this great vision.

My strength was to conceive and launch the vision. Then God called others to stand with us who could help organize, follow up, and carry the vision to completion. By myself I couldn't accomplish the work; I needed help. So God supernaturally connected me to team members I needed.

Mere words cannot express how very thankful I am to God for assembling such quality people to complement my gifts. Without them, I wouldn't have been able to accomplish all that we have done over the years. I had the passion and impetus to start these projects, but the advances we have made in so many realms of ministry wouldn't have been possible without the divine connections God had prearranged.

God knew that a multi-membered team was necessary to fulfill such a huge assignment. As Ecclesiastes 4:9,10 (*NLT*) says, "Two people are better off than one, for they can help each other succeed. If one person falls, the other can reach out and help. But someone who falls alone is in real trouble."

I want you to know that God also has divine connections awaiting *you* all along your life's journey. Sometimes when you least expect it, the Lord will surprise you by bringing you just the right person you need to help you do another part of what He has assigned for your life.

Such was the case in the life of the apostle Paul. As he adjusted his ministry to become more in sync with divinely revealed priorities, the Lord supernaturally connected him with special individuals who would help him fulfill his God-given vision. These divine connections were just as important for Paul's success as the supernatural financial provision God provided, which we covered in the last chapter.

> Sometimes when you least expect it, the Lord will surprise you by bringing you just the right person you need to help you do another part of what He has assigned for your life.

Money is a blessing, and it's necessary to fulfill your calling. But the manifestation of divine connections to build your team is a supernatural sign of God's approval on what you are doing.

PAUL MEETS AQUILA AND PRISCILLA

In Acts chapter 18, Paul arrived in the Gentile city of Corinth. Corinth was the next stop after Paul had preached with minimal results in Athens — a city "wholly given to idolatry" (Acts 17:16). Before his time in Athens, Paul had gone through all kinds of trials and endured great opposition, especially from hostile Jews, wherever he traveled. As we've seen, he had already been beaten, imprisoned, ridiculed, and chased out of cities and towns. As Paul made his way to Corinth, he must have felt very alone and discouraged, with no clear direction and no one to talk to about the things he'd been through or about what might be next in God's plan for his life.

Paul could have just sat down and said, "Well, that's it. I'm battle-scarred, and I'm tired. And for all my efforts to preach Jesus in Athens, I have very little fruit to show for it. Maybe my ministry is over." If Paul *had* responded that way to his discouraging circumstances, his conclusion may have seemed justified. But that isn't what he did. He just kept moving forward by God's grace, setting out for Corinth, and determining within himself to know nothing among those he preached to but "Jesus Christ, and him crucified" (1 Corinthians 2:2).

It should be the same in our lives. Even when we are facing truly difficult circumstances, we must choose *not* to get discouraged or to respond negatively to what we're facing.

That's not to say that in the midst of heavy trials, we can't ask the questions that are in our hearts concerning God's perfect will for our lives. As I explained, we might need to hear afresh and anew God's exact plan and course — and align or *realign* ourselves with that. Or we might simply need to stay the course and take hold of the manifold grace of God that He liberally supplies on our behalf. But whatever the case, quitting is not an option.

You see, *the way we respond to a crisis determines what happens next*. For Paul, "what happened next" was a divinely appointed meeting with Aquila and Priscilla. Paul's point of crisis became a place of revelation concerning his ministry. And through the many epistles he was subsequently inspired by the Holy Spirit to write, Paul's ministry and the Scriptures he penned still speak to us today.

Shortly before or perhaps at nearly the same time that Paul arrived in Corinth, Aquila and Priscilla also entered the ancient port city for the first time. This husband-and-wife team had just experienced a very discouraging ordeal themselves, having been ordered to leave their home in the city of Rome.

> *The way we respond to a crisis determines what happens next.*

The Emperor Claudius had recently issued an edict to expel Jews from Rome — an imperial decree that especially impacted Jewish believers. One early Roman historian named Suetonius wrote that the reigning emperor had displaced Jews who "were constantly inciting tumults under their leader Christos."[3] Many historians believe the edict was a reaction to the opposition in the Jewish community against the rising influence of Jewish Christians who were preaching Christ.

It was a sudden, tragic turn of events when Aquila and Priscilla and others were forcefully ejected from their home because of religious persecution. We're not sure how the event unfolded, but this type of imperial edict was often carried out in an abrupt and harsh manner during early New Testament times. It's very possible that the Roman military burst into this couple's home one night, destroyed many of their possessions, drove them out on the street, and ordered them to get out of town. Not only that, but it's a good possibility that those marshaled forces also

---

[3]*Lives of Caesars*, Claudius, 25.4.

confiscated the couple's legal documents, stripped them of many legal rights, and took away most of their money.

So Aquila and Priscilla had begun traveling east — not by *choice*, but rather by *force*. They very likely had no time to tell their families or their fellow church members good-bye. In one fell swoop, they had been evicted from their home, isolated from Roman society, and ejected from their home country. This represented an enormous loss for Aquila and Priscilla financially, mentally, emotionally, and socially. And certainly it was a great loss to them spiritually as well, for they had been forcibly and suddenly severed from their church congregation.

From their home in Rome, Aquila and Priscilla headed for the nearest port, where they boarded a ship that would ultimately take them to Corinth. When they finally arrived in the city, they must have felt defeated and dejected. The Bible doesn't tell us whether the couple intended to stay there. Perhaps they had planned to walk to the other side of the city and board another ship to another Grecian port.

But as these two walked the streets of this unfamiliar city, most likely feeling deflated and discouraged, they just "happened" to meet the apostle Paul, who had just arrived in Corinth from Athens. Life for all three of them was about to change drastically.

THE LORD ORDERS OUR STEPS

God was in no way the instigator of Aquila and Priscilla's disastrous departure from Rome. But He is the God who knows the end from the beginning (*see* Isaiah 46:10) and who "…works all things according to the counsel of His will" (Ephesians 1:11 *NKJV*). God was ordering the steps of these three Gospel preachers when they weren't even aware of it.

Acts 18:1,2 talks about this supernatural meeting in the city of Corinth and the difficult circumstances that Aquila and Priscilla had endured shortly before that meeting:

> **After these things Paul departed from Athens, and came to Corinth; and found a certain Jew named Aquila, born in Pontus, lately come from Italy, with his wife Priscilla; (because that Claudius had commanded all Jews to depart from Rome:) and came unto them.**

Aquila and Priscilla most likely had never even heard of the apostle Paul. They weren't looking for him, and Paul wasn't looking for Aquila and Priscilla. But when the paths of these three crossed on the streets of Corinth, it quickly became apparent to them all that it was a divine connection. The Lord had orchestrated the meeting supernaturally, bringing these three people from different parts of the world to converge *in the same city, on the same spot, at the same time* for the furtherance of His plan and purposes.

Only God can do something like that. And I want to encourage you today that even when you're going through difficult times in your own life, He will do the same for you as you trust Him each day for guidance and direction. God will put you in the right place at the right time, and He will connect you with the right people so you can fulfill His plan and will for your life.

> **God will put you in the right place at the right time, and He will connect you with the right people so you can fulfill His plan and will for your life.**

That's one of the miraculous things that happens when we align ourselves with the plans and purposes of God for our lives. He divinely connects us with the exact people we need on our team to fulfill our part in His plan.

PAUL 'FOUND'
HIS FUTURE TEAM MEMBERS

In Acts 18:2, the Scripture tells us that Paul "found" Aquila and Priscilla as they were entering the city. The word "found" is the Greek word *heurisko*, and it carries an element of surprise. It literally means, *"I found it!"* It's where we get our word *eureka*. By using this word, the writer of Acts tells us of the *great elation* this threesome felt when they met each other providentially, or by God's divine direction.

Imagine the unexpected delight Paul experienced when he met two other Gospel preachers while entering one of the world's most wicked cities. For him to find Aquila and Priscilla at that moment in that exact place was such an unexpected, joyous blessing that Paul didn't have words to express it. We can only imagine what an infusion of strength and encouragement it was for the apostle to realize he had just gained such powerful comrades for his team. It was a *eureka* moment!

Verse 2 also says Aquila and Priscilla had come "lately" from Italy. This Greek word was used in Greek culture to describe meat that was just *freshly killed*. The use of this term indicates that Aquila and Priscilla had "freshly" come to Corinth, just as Paul had. This assures us that all three of them were new arrivals. Some expositors say it's possible the couple met the apostle Paul as all three of them were making their way into the city for the first time.

The verse goes on to say that Paul "...came unto them." That means when Paul found Aquila and Priscilla, he formed a *partnership* with them. The apostle was immediately aware that this wasn't an accidental coincidence but a divine plan strategically put in place by the Holy Spirit for this specific time and setting. As we've seen, Paul was in the city where a shift of focus took place in his ministry that aligned him more closely to God's priorities for his life. Meanwhile, the Lord had been faithful to do His part, supernaturally guiding people to connect with Paul in order to help him build the supernatural team he would need to fulfill the huge assignment God had called him to accomplish.

GOD CAN CAUSE ALL THINGS TO WORK TOGETHER FOR YOUR GOOD

When Aquila and Priscilla had first entered Corinth, their eviction from Rome was still very fresh in their memories. They entered the city still working through the grief they had felt as they were forced to pack up what they could take of their belongings and leave behind their lives in Rome against their will.

That had indeed been a tragic event in the lives of Aquila and Priscilla. But it also proved the truth Paul later wrote to the church of Rome in Romans 8:28: "And we know that all things work together for good to them that love God, to them who are the called according to his purpose."

> The apostle was immediately aware that this wasn't an accidental coincidence but a divine plan strategically put in place by the Holy Spirit for this specific time and setting.

After the couple's heartbreaking expulsion from Rome, it looked like all was lost for Aquila and Priscilla — but not in God's eyes. That eviction put them on the road to Corinth, where they met Paul and started the most brilliant phase of their ministry. It would be a phase that outshone anything they had left behind in Rome.

What began as a tragedy became the very means by which a new team was created that would propel the Gospel into new lands. Aquila and Priscilla entered the city of Corinth and joined with Paul, making them one of the greatest apostolic teams in history. Working side by side with the apostle Paul, they helped give birth to the church of Corinth — a congregation that would become a powerful and significant influence for God's Kingdom throughout the lands of Greece.

A DIVINELY DESIGNED TEAM
TO FULFILL A DIVINE PURPOSE

During the years that Paul, Aquila, and Priscilla were growing up in their separate parts of the world, God was already well aware that they would one day surrender their lives in the service of His Son, intersect in the city of Corinth, and work together to build His Church. A divine process was already underway during the adolescent years of this threesome, completely unbeknownst to each of them. God was preparing and equipping each with the skills they would need one day to operate as an effective team with a single cause — the advancement of His Kingdom.

Think of it. In Paul's wildest imagination, he would never have expected to meet two Christian ministers in the rampantly pagan city of Corinth — but he did! Then on top of that, both Aquila and Priscilla were Jews, which was an added blessing to Paul because he had roots in the very same culture. When the three of them met, they could speak Hebrew to each other; they didn't have to speak Greek or Latin. They also all shared a call of God on their lives for ministry. *And* they shared a skill and a trade in common: "And because he [Paul] was of the same *craft*, he abode with them, and wrought: for by their occupation they were tentmakers" (Acts 18:3).

Verse 3 may not sound very powerful, but there is so much in this verse. Let's read the first part of it again: "And because he was of the same *craft*...." The word "craft" is the Greek word *tekhnos*. It's where we get the word for *technology*. "And because he was of the same craft [technology], he abode with them, and wrought: for by their occupation they were tentmakers."

As I shared in the last chapter, the Greek word for "tentmaker" referred not only to the profession of *making tents*, but also at times to *making cloaks, curtains, shoes, or any products made from leather*. Paul was raised in the manner of all Jewish boys, who were customarily taught some kind of a trade as children. For Paul, his trade was tentmaking. Whether or not his craft included leather-work, we can't be sure. But we do know that Paul originally came from Cilicia, a region of the world where there were huge herds of a certain breed of goats. The hair of this breed was very durable and was used to make tents in New Testament times. Aquila was also taught tentmaking as a trade when he was a boy. He grew up on the southern coast of the Black Sea, where this same breed of goats was raised and herded.

These two young boys were raised in different parts of Asia Minor with no knowledge of each other's existence. Taught the craft of tentmaking as children, the two boys never dreamed they'd grow up to one day meet someone else skilled in the same craft who would become a key partner in life — not only in tentmaking, but in a much greater pursuit. They didn't know God would one day use the earnings from their common skills to establish a work for His Kingdom in a pagan city far from home.

But God knew! He knew these two young men would meet on that road in Corinth. God knew the precise moment they would meet — the exact date and time — and He knew this even when Paul and Aquila were children. These two boys weren't raised as Christians. Yet even when they didn't know Jesus, He was gifting and equipping them, giving them the training they needed so that one day when they met in Corinth, they could work together in a practical way to make money for the work of the ministry.

The skeptic might try to convince himself that this moment when Paul, Aquila, and Priscilla crossed paths and met each other for the first time was a coincidence. But it was God's strategic design all along! He was turning the devil's past attacks against these three believers to their favor! And in the days and months that followed, that team would partner together to establish one of the greatest, strongest churches of the New Testament.

Paul and Aquila never knew as young men that their lives would one day intersect, but *God* did! The same is true in *our* lives. God often works in ways we don't see or recognize as His plan in order to prepare and equip us for what He knows is ahead.

> God often works in ways we don't see or recognize as His plan in order to prepare and equip us for what He knows is ahead.

Often we don't have the foggiest idea what God is doing. But He knows *everything* about our lives from beginning to end, and He is always working behind the scenes to help bring us into the fullness of all He has planned for us. He knows our thoughts before we think them and our words before we speak them (*see* Psalm 139:2,4). David wrote about this omniscient aspect of God's character: "You saw me before I was born. Every day of my life was recorded in your book. Every moment was laid out before a single day had passed" (Psalm 139:16 *NLT*).

Just think of all the ways the Lord has led you in times past that have prepared you for where you are right now. At the time, you probably weren't even aware He was preparing you for something. Perhaps you worked at a job you really didn't like. You may have been asked to complete tasks you didn't want to do. You may not have understood at the time, but later you looked back at that job and thought, *I can see how God was working to prepare me for what I'm doing today.*

Well, if that's what God did for you in the past, you can be confident that He is equipping you *right now* for what's ahead in your future. So keep your heart open to Him. Be happy and joyful that He's working in your life. Know with certainty that He has a *good* plan for you (*see* Jeremiah 29:11) and that He is working out that plan, even when you don't understand what's going on.

FERVENT COWORKERS

Acts 18:3 reveals another important fact about the divine connection between Aquila and Priscilla and the apostle Paul. It says, "…He abode with them, and *wrought*…." This word "wrought" is the Greek word *ergadzomai*, which comes from the root word *ergos*, meaning *work*. When *ergos* becomes the word *ergadzomai*, its meaning expands to depict someone *working energetically*.

In other words, Paul, Aquila, and Priscilla knew how to swing into action! When they all arrived in Corinth, they had a common cause — to preach the Gospel of Jesus Christ — and they *energetically worked* with all their hearts to fulfill the call of God on their lives.

> When God divinely connects you with the right people, they will be like fuel on the fire to help motivate you to fulfill His will for your life.

When God divinely connects you with the right people, they will be like fuel on the fire to help motivate you to fulfill His will for your life. This spiritual principle is echoed in Proverbs 27:17 (*NLT*): "As iron sharpens iron, so a friend sharpens a friend." That's one of the functions of those called by God to come alongside to help you. They will actually *energize* you to pursue the call with even greater fervency than before.

Consider your connection with certain key individuals in your life. Do you know in your heart that your initial encounter with them was orchestrated by God to help you fulfill His plan and purposes? If so, you can count it as evidence that you're on track with His plan for your life.

The Architect
Doesn't Build the House Alone

Notice again that God didn't bring Paul to Corinth to minister by *himself*. Even with Paul's anointing, his great giftings, and his breadth of knowledge, he wasn't capable of taking on the city of Corinth by himself. The apostle needed the gifts and callings that the Lord had placed on other people as well — people like Aquila and Priscilla. So God led the couple to cross paths with Paul, and a divinely empowered partnership was formed.

But there's one more thing I don't want you to miss. In First Corinthians 3:10, Paul revealed his particular role in the building of the Corinthian church:

> **According to the grace of God which is given unto me, as a wise *masterbuilder*, I have laid the foundation, and another buildeth thereon. But let every man take heed how he buildeth thereupon.**

The word "masterbuilder" is the Greek word *architekton,* which is where we get our word *architect*, and the word "wise" is the Greek word *sophos*, meaning *one who has special insight.* So in this verse, Paul is saying, *"I was the architect for this church, and as the architect, I had the special insight — divine revelation — to know how to lay its foundation and how to build its structure...."*

But this leads me to ask a question: What do architects do? They produce blueprints. They generate vision; they design the plan; and they put the plan on paper. They know every requirement and code to make a building stand strong and function properly. They are gifted for the building process.

But how many architects do you know who can also actually pour concrete or install electric wiring and plumbing? I personally don't know one. Yes, architects are gifted to design and oversee the plan, but they don't actually insert themselves into the building process and physically construct the building. They work with a construction team to build the structures they visualize and design.

Spiritually, the apostle Paul had supernatural insight to know how the church at Corinth should be built. However, he was not capable of completing the divine construction project alone. It would require the varied skills of a team to make the dream of that church become a reality, and that's why God orchestrated Paul's connection with Aquila and Priscilla. Paul was the architect, the team leader, but God assembled a spiritual "construction crew" to help him actually produce what he could spiritually visualize in Corinth.

> Paul was the architect, the team leader, but God assembled a spiritual "construction crew" to help him actually produce what he could spiritually visualize in Corinth.

GOD WILL SEND YOU DIVINE CONNECTIONS

Let this scriptural example be an anchor of encouragement to you as you follow God's will for your life. When you know what

God has called you to do and you're walking it out to the best of your ability, He will faithfully connect you with the right people at the right time to help you successfully fulfill the assignment. God will do whatever is required to assemble the assistance you need to obey Him — even if He has to guide people from across the world to where you are.

Denise and I were not sufficiently equipped by ourselves to fulfill God's will for our lives in the former Soviet Union. We needed other God-called people to help us do what we were not equipped to do.

You may be the pastor of a church, a leader of a ministry, or the manager of a business. Whatever God has assigned you to do, it is essential that you recognize from the outset that you can't do it all by yourself. You're not gifted to do everything that is needed to bring your God-given vision to pass. You're just anointed to do *your* part.

> Whatever God has assigned you to do, it is essential that you recognize from the outset that you can't do it all by yourself. You're just anointed to do *your* part.

We are the Body of Christ. A person's physical body is more than a head. He also has hands, arms, legs, feet, eyes, ears, and many internal organs that are unseen. All parts work together for the proper function of the body as a whole.

The same is true with Christ's spiritual Body of believers. As Paul stated, "...We are fellow workmen (joint promoters, *laborers together*) with and for God..." (1 Corinthians 3:9 *AMPC*).

I want to encourage you today to be open to God and allow Him to bring divinely designed appointments with key people into your life — in your career, in your ministry, in *every area* of your life. He will do the same for you as He did for the apostle

Paul and has done for countless other believers through the centuries. Just trust Him each day for guidance and direction, even when you're going through difficult times. God will put you in the right place at the right time, and He will connect you with precisely the right people so you can *fully* accomplish His plan for your life — all the way to the finish line of your spiritual race!

THINK ABOUT IT

1. When Paul met Aquila and Priscilla, it was with great joy. He had found people who walked and talked like him and shared the same passion for Christ.

   Are there people you've met along your journey in life who have been like Aquila and Priscilla to you — whose companionship has been like a breath of fresh air as you labor to obey God's will for your life? Set aside some time to truly consider the intentional, strategic intersections with key people in your life that reveal God's hand helping you stay on course to fulfill your divine assignment.

2. Have you ever experienced times in your life that you didn't like or understand? Often God uses experiences in our lives to prepare and equip us for the tasks ahead. Take a few moments to look back over some of the difficult times you have had to overcome in your past. Ask God to show you how He used those situations to mold and make you into the person you are today, thereby equipping you to do His will.

3. We all want divine connections — individuals who are answers to specific prayers we've lifted before the Lord. *But you are a divine connection for someone else* — you are *their* answer to prayer! So consider this: What individuals has God strategically placed around you for whom you have the gifts and talents to help? In what practical ways can you be a blessing of strength to *their* lives? Pray and ask God for His wisdom. Remember, what you plant in the lives of others, you will reap in your own life (*see* Galatians 6:7).

CHAPTER NINE

DIVINE PROTECTION IN THE CENTER OF GOD'S WILL

*F*rom Genesis to Revelation, God promises to protect you from all the plots and plans of the enemy. It doesn't mean the enemy won't try to attack, or that unfortunate events will not try to assault you, but Scripture declares that "the eyes of the Lord search the whole earth in order to strengthen those whose hearts are fully committed to him…" (2 Chronicles 16:9 *NLT*). This is a promise you can lay claim to for your life!

As your Divine Protector:

- God is your *"Hiding Place"* (*see* Psalm 32:7) — preserving you from trouble and surrounding you with songs of deliverance.

- God is your *"Strong Tower"* (*see* Proverbs 18:10) — a fortified place of safety for you to run into.

- God is your *"Shield"* (*see* Psalm 3:3; 33:20) — to help you in hard times, lifting your head when you are down and producing His glory in your life.

- God is your *"Mountain"* (*see* Psalm 125:2) — surrounding you as the mountains surround and protect Jerusalem.

The Scriptures are replete with God's promises to protect you and to keep you (*see* Numbers 6:24-26). As we consider the protective care of God over your life, let's once again look at the life of the apostle Paul to see what happens when you're in the center of God's will as it pertains to divine protection.

Don't Let the Enemy Scare You Out of God's Will

We discussed in Chapter Seven the events that occurred when Paul first arrived in Corinth. He once again went to the synagogue and spent time ministering the Gospel to the Jewish community, as he had in times past. But this time the audience in the synagogue also included Gentiles who were open-minded and had a heart to hear what Paul had to say. Eventually the majority of the Jews rose up to oppose Paul and his message, as had so often been the case in times past. Paul's decision, as a result, to focus on the Gentiles in the city proved to be a turning point in his ministry. Acts 18:6 records the moment the apostle made that crucial decision that would dramatically affect the rest of his time in Corinth and, indeed, the course of his future ministry.

> **And when they opposed themselves, and blasphemed, he shook his raiment, and said unto them, Your blood be upon your own heads; I am clean: from henceforth I will go unto the Gentiles.**

From that moment onward, it seems Paul shifted his attention to the Gentiles as a first priority. As a result of this monumental decision, he began to experience a brand-new level of victory and success like he had never experienced previously in his ministry.

Part of Paul's early success in Corinth was the salvation of Crispus, the ruler of the Corinthian synagogue. This man was a significant Jew in the city and held a position of tremendous influence — not only in the lives of Jews, but also in the lives of Gentiles who were looking for a better way of life through a relationship with the one true God.

Indeed, this was a glorious victory for God's Kingdom. Not only was Crispus saved, but his wife, children, and servants were all born again as well. In addition, many other Corinthians were so impacted when they learned of this Jewish leader's conversion to Christ that they were also saved and baptized! Acts 18:8 says that many Corinthians believed when they heard of Crispus' conversion. This is a reference to the Gentile Corinthians who were amazed that even Crispus had become a Christian. If the leader of the synagogue had converted, these Gentiles concluded, surely the message of Christ must be true — and as a result, they also received Jesus as their Savior and Lord.

> **From that moment onward, it seems Paul shifted his attention to the Gentiles as a first priority. As a result of this monumental decision, he began to experience a brand-new level of victory and success like he had never experienced previously in his ministry.**

After Paul began to focus primarily on the Gentiles in alignment with the original call he had received in Acts 9:15, he began to experience success in his ministry like never before. Although an attempted strategy by hostile Corinthian Jews later tried to throw him off track, this time Paul experienced unusual favor to overcome each attack. And unlike past instances of persecution, Paul wasn't run out of Corinth. Instead, he was supernaturally protected, and he outlasted his opposition.

Likewise, you need to know that when you're finally positioned in the will of God, the devil will do his best to find a way to push you off course. He doesn't want you to stay on God's path for your life, so he will try to muster an attack against you to scare you away, to knock you off track, or to convince you to abandon God's direction for your life.

But you have God's promise that "...when the enemy comes in like a flood, the Spirit of the Lord will lift up a standard against him" (Isaiah 59:19 *NKJV*). As you will see, that's exactly what He did for Paul.

GOD PROMISES TO PROTECT YOU

When Paul became aware that the devil was attempting to abort what was happening in Corinth, the Lord brought a clear word to him:

> **...The Lord spoke to Paul in the night by a vision, "Do not be afraid, but speak, and do not keep silent; for I am with you, and no one will attack you to hurt you; for I have many people in this city."**
>
> **— Acts 18:9,10 *NKJV***

If you look carefully at this verse, you will see four key things the Lord spoke to Paul. First, He said, *"Do not be afraid, but speak."*

It's interesting to note that in all Paul's years of ministry up to that moment, this was the *first* time — at least the first time we have recorded — that he had ever heard the words, *"Do not fear"* from the Lord. When Paul shifted to the Gentiles as his primary focus, it appears that he also shifted to a new measure of divine protection. It wasn't going to be the same in Corinth as it had been in so many other cities during the early years of ministry, where he had suffered terribly at the hands of the Jewish zealots who opposed him. Paul had positioned himself to minister to the Gentiles first as a matter of priority. As a result, he discovered the protective hand of God like he'd never before experienced it in his life.

It's important to understand that being in the center of God's will doesn't mean you will escape all trouble. You can be sure that the devil will do his best to knock you off track, because that is his mode of operation. However, being in God's will does provide you with divine protection even in the *midst* of troubling situations. Certainly troubling times will come because causing trouble is what the devil always does. But although the devil will try to attack you — as was the case even during Paul's stay in Corinth — you will be surrounded with protection and favor to keep you safe as you navigate the storm.

So, first, the Lord said to the apostle Paul, "Do not be afraid." Second, He said to Paul, *"I am with you."* This is very similar to what the Lord spoke to Joshua after Moses died and Joshua had been chosen to lead the children of Israel into the Promised Land. The Lord said to Joshua, "No one will be able to stand against you as long as you live. For I will be with you as I was with Moses. I will not fail you or abandon you.... This is my command — be strong and courageous! Do not be afraid or discouraged. For the Lord your God is with you wherever you go" (Joshua 1:5,9 *NLT*).

When you're in the perfect will of God — in the right place, doing the right thing — you are assured an abiding sense of God's presence. God promised it to Joshua; He promised it to the apostle Paul; and He promises it to you and me as well. He is the same

> You can be sure that the devil will do his best to knock you off track, because that is his mode of operation. However, being in God's will does provide you with divine protection even in the *midst* of troubling situations.

yesterday, today, and forever (*see* Hebrews 13:8), and He never shows favoritism (*see* Romans 2:11).

But I want you to know that should you choose to veer from God's ordained path for your life, it is a lonely and vulnerable place. If you walk a path God didn't call you to walk, you will simply experience less protection than you would if you stayed on track with His calling on your life. Of course, His hand will always be upon you because you are in Christ. But if you choose to go in a direction different than God's revealed plan for you, you are giving the enemy unnecessary access, thereby placing yourself in jeopardy on many levels. However, all of this is avoidable by staying on track with His will for your life.

> You must determine to stay positioned right in the middle of God's revealed will for your life. In that place of obedience, you can have a rock-solid assurance that He will cover you — front, back, underneath, and on all sides!

That's why you must determine to stay positioned right in the middle of God's revealed will for your life. In that place of obedience, you can have a rock-solid assurance that He will cover you — front, back, underneath, and on all sides! He's your Guardian who never slumbers, as the psalmist declared:

Indeed, he who watches over Israel never slumbers or sleeps. The Lord himself watches over you! The Lord stands beside you as your protective shade. The sun will not harm you by day, nor the moon at night. The Lord keeps you from all harm and watches over your life. The Lord keeps watch over you as you come and go, both now and forever.

— Psalm 121:4-8 *NLT*

What an incredible promise of protection from God!

First, the Lord said to Paul, *"Do not fear."* Second, He said, *"I am with you."* Third, God said to Paul in this verse: *"No one will attack you to hurt you"* (v. 10). As we've seen, Paul had been hurt on *many* occasions prior to this — beaten, stoned and left for dead, and run out of many cities. He'd had enough of those experiences that he didn't want to repeat them. So when Satan tried to resurrect the agonizing memories of his previous experiences, Paul needed an assuring word from Heaven that it was not going to happen during his time in Corinth — and that assurance is what the Lord gave him.

Fourth, the Lord told Paul, *"I have many people in this city"* (v. 10). The people He was talking about were not just those who had already been saved, but many others who were yet to be saved. Paul's Heaven-assigned job was not finished — it wasn't time for him to leave town. The Corinthian church was not yet established, and if he had left at that moment, his departure would have been premature in God's plan.

When you're tempted to leave your present situation, you need to stop and ask yourself some soul-searching questions.

- *Have I finished the job God gave me to do?*

- *Have I completed every part of my divine assignment in this place?*

- *What will happen to the work if I leave now?*

- *Will souls be missed for eternity?*

- *Can I leave with a clear conscience, knowing in my heart that my job is complete?*

There may be moments in which you're tempted to be afraid and to flee from the place where you know God has assigned you for this season. But if you will quiet yourself and listen carefully, the Lord will speak to you, giving you a reassuring word of encouragement. If fear or pressure is in the picture, you can know that the Lord is not behind it. It's most likely the enemy pressuring you to abandon your God-given assignment.

Promises Are Often Put to the Test

God spoke a reassuring word to Paul, telling him, "...I am with you, and no one will attack you to hurt you..." (Acts 18:10 *NKJV*). It wasn't very long before this divine promise was put to the test. In Acts 18:12 and 13, Luke gave us some details of what happened to Paul as he was ministering:

> **And when Gallio was the deputy of Achaia, the Jews made insurrection with one accord against Paul, and brought him to the judgment seat, saying, This fellow persuadeth men to worship God contrary to the law.**

Notice the Bible says that the Jews made an "insurrection" against Paul "with one accord." Once again, Paul had problems with Jews who had not come to Christ. These hostile Jews instigated an "insurrection," stirring up a huge crowd to come against Paul with the intent to assault and harm him. The phrase "with one accord" in Greek carries the idea of something that had been carefully devised and then carried out by an angry religious mob.

Motivated by anger, jealousy, and lack of understanding, these unbelieving Jews physically carried Paul to the judgment seat of Gallio, who was the governor of the region at that time. Gallio's place of rule was located in the middle of the marketplace in central Corinth. What happened next was nothing short of an amazing display of God's powerful protection.

> **And when Paul was now about to open his mouth, Gallio said unto the Jews, If it were a matter of wrong or wicked lewdness, O ye Jews, reason would that I should bear with**

you: But if it be a question of words and names, and of your law, look ye to it; for I will be no judge of such matters. And he drave them from the judgment seat.

Acts 18:14-16

Remember the words God spoke to Paul in the middle of the night: *"…I am with you, and no one will attack you to hurt you…"* (v. 10 *NKJV*). In every previous experience before Corinth, the apostle had nearly gotten the life beaten out of him during such assaults by hostile Jews. But this time, Paul experienced divine protection beyond anything he had ever known in his ministry.

The unbelieving Jews took Paul to Gallio, intent on their mission to present their accusations to the governor and get Paul pronounced guilty and punished. But instead of having the apostle beaten, Gallio basically replied, "I don't want anything to do with this" — and then he drove them all from his court.

The word "drave" in verse 16 comes from a Greek phrase indicating that the Jewish leaders probably lingered and tried to pressure Gallio into inflicting some sort of punishment on Paul. They probably pleaded, "Please do *something* to punish this man!" But Gallio would not hear of it.

Verse 17 says, "Then all the Greeks took Sosthenes, the chief ruler of the synagogue, and beat him before the judgment seat. And Gallio cared for none of those things." In essence, Gallio shut his eyes and let the Gentiles of Corinth beat Sosthenes, who apparently was the new ruler of the synagogue after Crispus. Sosthenes was also the very person who had led the charge to bring Paul to the judgment seat and plead for *him* to be beaten!

Don't miss the significance of this, because it reveals a spiritual law in operation. Sosthenes, the chief ruler of the synagogue, would have been the leader of the crowd who had sought to dig a trap for Paul. But Paul was divinely protected, and *Sosthenes* fell into the very trap he himself had dug (*see* Proverbs 28:10). Meanwhile, Paul walked away without one scratch on his body, ministry, or reputation.

A closer look at the story reveals a twist of divine irony that played out in the aftermath of this high drama. Sometime after Sosthenes was beaten that day, he got saved! We see evidence of this remarkable development in the very beginning of Paul's first letter to the Corinthian church, where he wrote, "Paul called to be an apostle of Jesus Christ through the will of God, and *Sosthenes our brother*."

Most scholars agree that this was the same Jewish leader who tried to instigate an insurrection against Paul and devise a strategy to harm him and then run him out of town! This was the man who led the hostile group of Jews to bring Paul before the high court so he could be punished as a criminal — and then became the one who was actually beaten that day. But it seems that in the months and years that followed, Sosthenes came to Christ and even became a traveling companion of the apostle Paul and a part of his apostolic team.

> **God can work miracles in even the hardest heart, so never underestimate the power of His grace to change a person's life — even your enemies.**

This tells me that people who have been your enemies in the past might end up your allies in the future. That's what the Bible teaches in Proverbs 16:7: "When a man's ways please the Lord, he maketh even his enemies to be at peace with him." God can work miracles in even the hardest heart, so never underestimate the power of His grace to change a person's life — even your enemies.

His Protection
Will Produce Peace and Fruitfulness

Through it all, the apostle Paul experienced an extended period of peace and success in ministry in Corinth. Acts 18:18 reveals that "...Paul after this tarried there [in Corinth] yet a good while, and then took his leave of the brethren, and sailed thence into Syria, and with him Priscilla and Aquila...." How long did Paul stay in Corinth? Verse 11 says that "he continued there a year and six months, teaching the word of God among them."

This was the longest stay in one city that Paul had ever experienced anywhere up to that point in his ministry. Throughout that year and a half, the Lord was with him to protect him. No man set a hand on the apostle to hurt him while he resided in Corinth. Paul was reaching the harvest of souls he was supposed to reach, and as a result, he experienced a new measure of divine provision, protection, favor, and blessing.

Again, *knowing* and *being in* the will of God is the key to success. From that moment forward, Paul would establish influential churches not only in Corinth, but in Ephesus, throughout the province of Asia, and in other parts of the Roman Empire. Although Paul would continue to attempt to reach the Jews out of his deep love for them, his priority had shifted to the Gentile world. He had embraced his calling as the apostle to the Gentiles, and he would flourish in that God-ordained position.

Paul would still have to deal with troublemakers from time to time. However, during his time in Corinth and in the years that followed, his ministry was marked with an increase of divine protection in demonstration as he followed the Holy Spirit's leading every step of the way.

Even when Paul experienced attacks in those latter years of his ministry, it seems he was graced with unusual favor to protect him even in the midst of the onslaught. An example of this was the unusual grace and favor afforded Paul when he came under assault in Jerusalem. When the Jews attempted to beat and kill him, divine intervention occurred and his life was spared. When the angry mob of Jews determined again to kill Paul, the local military commander ordered that he be surrounded with 200 soldiers, 70 horsemen, and 200 spearmen to transport him from Jerusalem to Caesarea. These forces were ordered to bring Paul "safely" to the palatial residence of the governor at the seaside (*see* Acts 23:23,24).

Once in Caesarea, Paul was held in a seaside palatial residence, in a room that some scholars say overlooked the gorgeous, man-made harbor that was world-famous. In Paul's room, he likely had a marvelous view, enjoyed the sea breeze, and could watch as ships sailed in and out of the harbor. From his room's view, he would also have been able to enjoy watching the races in the city's hippodrome that was located just a short distance away. Paul was supernaturally protected and blessed to live in the finest palace in Caesarea, even when he was under assault!

For two years, Paul experienced this remarkable treatment, confined in a palace rather than in a dingy prison. Was this the normal procedure of treatment for a prisoner? No, this was God's favor and divine protection in demonstration, even in the midst of an attack!

When Jews from Jerusalem finally attempted to bring charges against Paul, Felix gave the order for Paul to be protected from their aggression. What's even more amazing is that Felix gave the order for the centurion of the palace to protect Paul the entire time the apostle was held captive there. This arrangement also ensured that Paul's friends and family could freely come and go to visit him and that they could provide financially and materially all that he needed with no restrictions (*see* Acts 24:23). Acts 24:23 tells us that Paul had so much money available to him that Felix even hoped to receive an amount of money from Paul (*see* v. 26).

How much money did Paul have at his disposal that a nobleman like Felix would be impressed and hope to get some of it? Is this the normal condition of a prisoner? Of course not, but this demonstrates that even when Paul was under attack and held as a prisoner, he was provided for and supernaturally protected.

Although being held as a prisoner in Caesarea for two years was not the best scenario, Paul lived in a palatial residence, supernaturally protected and provided for the entire time he was held there in his seaside room with a view. He had the attention of soldiers, governors, kings — and eventually even that of an emperor in Rome.

When Paul was eventually transported to Rome, still as a prisoner, once again he was housed in his own rented dwelling for two years, where he freely received anyone who wanted to visit him (*see* Acts 28:30). Rome was the capital of the Roman Empire, and property was extremely expensive. A study of ancient homes, as well as of houses that were leased long-term and large enough to accommodate a number of visitors (since Paul received many visitors during that two-year period) reveals that such houses were astronomically expensive to rent. Yet Paul was able to pay two years' rent for a property in this category in the city of Rome. This was most assuredly *not* a normal situation for a Roman prisoner who would have little to none of the necessary funds personally available to secure this caliber of accommodation.

We also saw earlier in Chapter Three that Paul even experienced a certain level of protection in the way he was eventually executed. Because he was a Roman citizen, the apostle was subjected to a relatively expedient method of execution compared to the more common, grueling methods of Roman execution, such as crucifixion or burning at the stake.

To summarize, there is a pattern in Paul's latter years of ministry that can't be denied: Paul consistently experienced remarkable divine favor, provision, and protection, even in the midst of bad situations, that allowed him to produce supernatural fruit for God's Kingdom. These benefits defined Paul's latter years of ministry, all the way to the end when it was time for the apostle to say, "I have fought a good fight, I have finished my course, I have kept the faith" (2 Timothy 4:7).

STAY PUT WHERE GOD PLACED YOU

> God is your Divine Protector! All He asks is that you "stay put" in the center of His will where He has called you — *refusing* to move or give up and rejecting every scare tactic of the enemy to abdicate your post.

God is your Divine Protector! He is your *Hiding Place*, your *Strong Tower*, your *Shield*, and the *Mountain* that surrounds your life! He promises to be with you at all times and to *never* abandon you (*see* Hebrews 13:5). All He asks is that you "stay put" in the center of His will where He has called you — *refusing* to move or give up and rejecting every scare tactic of the enemy to abdicate your post.

As you stay put in the center of His will, you will be able to declare with David:

For in the time of trouble He shall hide me in His pavilion; in the secret place of His tabernacle He shall hide me; He shall set me high upon a rock.

And now my head shall be lifted up above my enemies all around me; therefore I will offer sacrifices of joy in His tabernacle; I will sing, yes, I will sing praises to the Lord.

— Psalm 27:5,6 *NKJV*

I encourage you to stay in God's will. If you're determined to stand where He has planted you and you refuse to budge from His revealed will for your life, you, too, will experience the reality of divine favor, abundant provision, and supernatural protection.

THINK ABOUT IT

1. God's divine protection is not just available to a few elite groups of believers — it is available to whosoever will call upon the name of the Lord and do His will.

   Take a few moments to reflect on your life. Describe at least one situation in which the Lord divinely protected you from the enemy. How does this memory of God's faithfulness in the past encourage you to trust Him in the present?

2. Nothing but the Word of God will renew your mind and establish a rock-solid knowing that God is your Guardian who will protect you at all times. Using a Bible concordance or an online search engine, find and write out at least three scriptures confirming God's divine protection and commit them to memory. (Hint: Read each verse in a few different versions of the Bible; choose the verses that "come alive" in your heart when you read them.)

3. Has the enemy bombarded your mind with fearful thoughts in an effort to get you to walk away from God's will? If so, you are not alone. Get quiet before the Lord and enter the "secret place" of His presence in prayer. Ask Him to strengthen you to not abandon your post and to empower you to trust in His divine protection as He promised. Write down any actions that you sense He is prompting you to take at this time.

Chapter Ten

LEARN TO SEE EVERY CRISIS AS A NEW OPPORTUNITY

*F*or the remainder of this book, I want to help you focus on the importance of *sustaining momentum in the pursuit of your call.* We'll talk about how to deal with and defeat the enemy's attacks. We'll discuss what it takes to stay unyielding to pressure that tries to derail you from God's plan and what's required to maintain a right heart attitude. But first, let's focus on this thought: *It's so important that you see every crisis as a new opportunity.*

Not one of us is immune to trouble while we live on this earth. So it's likely that at one time or another, you have felt so discouraged by some crisis in your life that you thought, *Everything around me looks hopeless and bleak, and the days ahead seem anything but bright.* It can be difficult to focus on the future when present circumstances seem to descend like a fog that obscures your spiritual view.

> It can be difficult to focus on the future when present circumstances seem to descend like a fog that obscures your spiritual view.

But I'm telling you right now that whatever you may be facing today, it didn't take God by surprise! If you stay faithful to do what He tells you to do and refuse to let go of His hand, He will lead you on a path that will take you straight out of the crisis and into His plan for your life. I promise you, the fog *will* eventually lift, and you'll bask in the glorious light of day, right in the middle of God's perfect will!

A CRISIS THAT BECAME
A DIVINE OPPORTUNITY

We learned in Chapter Eight how Aquila and Priscilla were suddenly ejected by imperial decree from their home in Rome. We can only imagine the tumultuous emotions this couple experienced as they headed to the nearest port and boarded a ship that would ultimately take them to Corinth. For them, Corinth presented a brand-new culture with new rules, new challenges, new faces, and very few Jews. This couple knew that they would be surrounded by pagans, and they had no knowledge of even one Christian in the entire city!

If you've ever moved from one culture to another, you know it can be a very difficult transition. It was made even more difficult for Aquila and Priscilla because it was a transition that was forced on them by Roman authorities rather than by their own choosing.

This ordeal was a major crisis for Aquila and Priscilla. Having lost everything — their home, their material possessions, their finances, and their familiar relationships — the couple embarked on the journey to an unfamiliar destination. It hadn't been in their plans to move to Corinth. They surely didn't choose to be there. Ejected from their home in Rome, their only immediate prospect was to live like refugees in a rampantly pagan city.

Let's think further about the plight of Aquila and Priscilla. They were Jews, but their faith was Christian, not Jewish. That means they arrived in Corinth with a tainted reputation even among their own people. To the local pagan population, they were outcasts as members of a suspect religious cult (Christianity) who had lost all their rights in the eyes of the Roman government. To the Jewish population in Corinth, Aquila and Priscilla also would have been held at arm's length by those suspicious of the growing number of "Jesus followers" who called themselves Christians.

Circumstances were against this couple. Pagan culture was against them. The opinion of their Jewish peers was against them. They had no money. They had no home. They needed a job and a place to live, but they likely didn't have the proper documentation to obtain either. Yet God worked through this unfortunate situation and used this displaced couple to help start one of the greatest churches in the entire New Testament!

I encourage you to let the story of Aquila and Priscilla bring you hope in the midst of your own crisis or in light of your past failures. Whatever situation you find yourself in, God can still use you, just as He used this couple. In God, there is hope for all who seek Him and get in the center of His will for their lives.

What had happened to Aquila and Priscilla was not an easy situation to go through. It's very probable that they had no idea they were headed to the right place in God's plan for them as they left their home in Rome.

But God knows the end from the beginning (*see* Isaiah 46:10), and He is always working on our behalf to help us fulfill His plan and purpose for our lives. The enemy may throw obstacles in our path to try to derail us, but the Lord is always able to turn all for the good as we put our trust in Him (*see* Romans 8:28).

> The enemy may throw obstacles in our path to try to derail us, but the Lord is always able to turn all for the good as we put our trust in Him.

When Aquila and Priscilla arrived at that right place, they found provision. They found purpose. They found favor and divine connections. It didn't matter how many strikes were against them — they had landed in the place where God wanted them to be. They had stepped into a new season, right in the center of His will, and their crisis became a major opportunity for God to manifest His glory through their lives.

THE GREATEST OPPORTUNITY IN HISTORY LIES BEFORE US!

All of us who are alive at the present moment find ourselves in a challenging moment in history. Some see it as a time of darkness and crisis. But if we allow God to change the way we think, we'll realize that it is also a time of great opportunity!

Since it's the context within which every one of us are living and pursuing God's will for our lives, let's pause in our discussion of Aquila and Priscilla for a moment to address this present hour we live in. The truth is, each of us should be able to identify with Aquila and Priscilla's crisis situation, because every day we are walking out a real-life experience of what we're talking about in this chapter. As believers living in this generation, we are called to learn how to make this crisis moment in God's timeline into a great opportunity — not only in our own lives personally, but also in the Church at large.

> As believers living in this generation, we are called to learn how to make this crisis moment in God's timeline into a great opportunity — not only in our own lives personally, but also in the Church at large.

Isaiah 60:1,2 says: "Arise, shine; for thy light is come, and the glory of the

Lord is risen upon thee. For, behold, the darkness shall cover the earth, and gross darkness the people: but the Lord shall rise upon thee, and his glory shall be seen upon thee."

This verse tells us a time is coming when "gross darkness" will cover the earth and the people. But precisely in that moment of crisis, the Lord will rise upon us and His glory shall be seen upon us as never before!

I believe this pivotal moment in God's great plan is not far away — *in fact, it may be at the door.* And when it manifests, it will be the most glorious event imaginable! It will be so glorious that masses of people will be converted as a result of God's glory on the Church (*see* Isaiah 60:3-5)! This will be *revival* on a scale that causes every previous revival to pale in comparison. This is the last great move of God's Spirit that our hearts have been waiting for!

What will the condition of the world be at this time — that is, in the last of the last days? Second Timothy chapter 3 tells us it will not be a safe place in which to live. Jesus talked about these last days in Matthew 24:4-14, telling us of the earth-shaking events and other end-time signs that will occur. Earthquakes, wars, rumors of wars, pestilence, nations rising against nations — these are just some of the things we can expect to witness in the last days before Jesus returns. (For an in-depth discussion of what the world will look like in the last of the last days, I encourage you to read my book *Signs You'll See Just Before Jesus Comes*).

Jesus taught us that the world would experience birth pangs like a woman preparing to have a baby. The closer we get to the end, the greater and more frequent those pangs will become. Paul confirmed this in Romans 8:20-22 (*NKJV*) when he wrote that the earth itself is groaning and travailing in pain for her final deliverance:

For the creation was subjected to futility, not willingly, but because of Him who subjected it in hope; because the creation itself also will be delivered from the bondage of corruption into the glorious liberty of the children of God. For we know that the whole creation groans and labors with birth pangs together until now.

These are the days in which God has ordained us to live! And amidst every crisis, He is providing opportunities to show His glory.

When I watch the news, I find it almost overwhelming to see the violence, moral decadence, political ugliness, financial crises, and daily, world-threatening changes that are occurring in different parts of the planet. Most of us wouldn't question that the world has become a *far different* place than the one we grew up in. In fact, sometimes it seems that things are just spinning out of control.

- Morals are snowballing in a downward direction.

- World leaders are scrambling to avoid a total collapse of the world financial markets, while predictions increase every day that such a crisis is just around the corner.

- The volatile political scene in the Middle East seems to become more and more unstable from day to day.

- Television has become a weapon for progressive liberals to attack nearly every principle of Christianity, with blasphemy and disrespect blatantly broadcasted over the airwaves on a continual basis.

It's clear we are living in the end times — what Paul called "perilous times" in his second letter to Timothy (*see* 2 Timothy 3:1). The Holy Spirit gave us a forewarning that this would be a difficult, dangerous time to live in so we could be prepared. We *must* be led by the Holy Spirit as we draw closer to the end of the age.

To many, these days will be a time of great *crisis* — the greatest crisis the world has ever known. At the same time, they will be days of the greatest *opportunity* for believers to advance God's Kingdom!

The Holy Spirit Has Warned Us About What Is Coming

We knew the end times would be challenging, but it has been difficult to imagine that things could change so quickly! However, as mentioned earlier, the Holy Spirit alerted us nearly 2,000 years ago that such times would come. Second Timothy 3:1 says, "This know also, that in the last times, perilous times shall come."

The word "know" in this verse is the Greek word *ginosko*, which means *to know something definitely and emphatically*. But the tense used with this word indicates that this is something so urgent that it *must* be known, *must* be recognized, and *must* be acknowledged.

In other words, what the Holy Spirit was about to say in the rest of this verse is *not* optional information to know and act on. He wanted us to really *know* it so we would be prepared and not caught off-guard when the things described in the following verses began to happen. The Holy Spirit was completely faithful to warn us in advance of what we should expect in the *very last of the last* days before Jesus' return.

> To many, these days will be a time of great *crisis* — the greatest crisis the world has ever known. At the same time, they will be days of the greatest *opportunity* for believers to advance God's Kingdom!

Then the Holy Spirit goes on to tell us what we *must* know — that "perilous times shall come." The word "perilous" comes from the Greek word *chalepos*, a word that described something that was *hurtful, harsh, cruel, ruthless, cutting, wounding,* and therefore *hard to bear.* It was frequently used to depict wild beasts that were *vicious, ferocious, fierce, unruly, uncontrollable, unpredictable,* and *dangerous.*

The word *chalepos* could also describe a geographical region that was filled with *risk* and *danger* and therefore should be avoided. In nearly every place where the word *chalepos* is used in ancient Greek texts, it encompasses the entire range of these meanings. If we took all these definitions into consideration, Second Timothy 3:1 could be interpreted: *"You must know that in the last days, periods of time that are hurtful, harmful, dangerous, unpredictable, uncontrollable, and high-risk will come...."*

The Holy Spirit faithfully warned us in advance that the last days would be hurtful, harsh, cruel, ruthless, cutting, and wounding — a time that will be hard for people to bear (*see* 2 Timothy 3:1). He told us that the world would become ferocious, fierce, unruly, uncontrollable, unpredictable, and dangerous. And He was actually alerting *our generation* that we would be the ones facing these *chalepos* times that no previous generation of Christians has yet confronted.

So What Are We To Do?

How should we respond to this forewarning? Shall we stay in our houses, close the blinds, and hide? What is the proper response to a world that seems to be sinking all around us?

First — we are to refuse to allow fear to grip our hearts!

Rather than hide in fear, we must learn to *use* these times as opportunities to reveal Jesus Christ to a lost world. We have hope and joy that the world doesn't have. We have knowledge about the future based on God's Word that the world cannot know. And even though the knowledge we've received doesn't always paint a rosy picture, we have confidence about the future that the lost world doesn't have.

All of this means you have a powerful opportunity to lead people to Jesus in the midst of these perilous times as you stay "...ready always to give an answer to every man that asketh you a reason of the hope that is in you..." (1 Peter 3:15). You are honored to live in this time of which God's prophets long foretold. And rather than running and hiding, you are called to follow Jesus' example when He once entered a particularly "*chalepos* territory" on Heaven's assignment.

When Jesus stepped out of the boat, He was met by two madmen who were terrorizing the people of the Gergesenes (*see* Matthew 8:23-34). Immediately Jesus recognized the danger and the undeniable demonic influence controlling the two men and used His God-given authority to *upend* the devil's hold on the situation. Casting out the demons in the men, Jesus set free that entire population from the fear that had paralyzed them for so long.

> **Rather than hide in fear, we must learn to *use* these times as opportunities to reveal Jesus Christ to a lost world.**

Jesus is our Example. *What terrified other people called Him to action.*

Others may have turned around, gotten back into their boat, and sailed away from that area. But Jesus knew He was called to that location at that moment to be a Source of deliverance. Had

He run away from that divine assignment, He would have missed the opportunity to set an entire region free. As "perilous" and as "exceedingly fierce" as those demonized men were, Jesus — led by the Spirit — nonetheless pressed forward with the supernatural weapons of God and transformed that situation to His glory.

Likewise, in these last days we live in — during what the Bible calls "perilous times" — the Holy Spirit beckons us as believers to step forward with the authority of Jesus Christ to bring deliverance, freedom, and peace to every person and every place where the devil has tried to bring chaos, danger, harshness, harm, and high-risk hazard. Not every person will receive the freedom that God wants to give him or her. Yet there are multitudes of people who *do* want it — and they are waiting for someone to bring them an answer to the chaos in their lives. It's time for us to do what Jesus did. We have to walk fearlessly in this world and let the power and glory of God flow through us!

> **Jesus is our Example.** *What terrified other people called Him to action.*

There's one more thing that all of us must do: We must submit our mouths to the Lordship of Jesus, asking Him to help us line up *our* words with *His* Word.

One day when I was praying, the Spirit of God spoke to me and said:

> *"Tell people to get the word 'crisis' out of their mouths. Their mouths will either bless them or defeat them — so if they keep saying the word 'crisis' over and over again, they will become ensnared and defeated by the words of their own mouths. They need to start declaring, 'OPPORTUNITY is all around me! There's never been a time of greater opportunity! This is the long-awaited time I've been praying and waiting for. I will be supernaturally blessed, supplied, and provided for in this*

season!' Again, tell people to get 'crisis' out of their mouths and to begin to say that this is their time of OPPORTUNITY!"

So refuse to cooperate with negativism, and instead make it your faith declaration that you are *not* participating in a crisis. In fact, you are *crisis-immune* because you are obedient to God's call and a giver into God's Kingdom. Declare that this is going to be the greatest season of opportunity you've ever experienced and that you will sail through this season with every need supernaturally supplied!

Yes, it's true that the world seems to be spinning out of control on many different fronts and that darkness is increasing. But this was prophesied 2,000 years ago by the Holy Spirit. You are not weaponless or powerless. The Holy Spirit's divine power has given you *all things* that pertain to life and godliness (*see* 2 Peter 1:3).

> **We must submit our mouths to the Lordship of Jesus, asking Him to help us line up *our* words with *His* Word.**

SEIZE THE OPPORTUNITY!

It's so important for you to learn to respond to crises in this manner, because your last crisis is *not* the very last one you're going to face! It's naïve to think that the devil is just going to lie down and watch you float from one victory to the next. Satan does *not* want you to succeed at fulfilling the will of God for your life, and he has purposed to do everything he can to sabotage your success.

Ephesians 5:16 says, "Redeeming the time, because the days are evil." The word "redeeming" means *to seize the opportunity* or *to take advantage of the time.* This is a pertinent word for us. We can choose never to be afraid of these times of crisis. We never have to be reduced to sitting in our homes inactive and worrying about what's going to happen in the days ahead.

This is our time to arise and shine! This is our time to work energetically as Paul did to fulfill God's will. *We must seize the opportunity and take advantage of these times to win the lost.* Especially because the days are evil, we have an opportunity to show people a better and a higher way and to make an eternal difference in their lives!

We were born at this time for a reason. We are chosen, anointed, and called to live for Jesus in these perilous times. We must lay hold of God's promises and rise up in this hour to let our light shine. We must wake up and realize that we are closing the age! We were chosen for this hour — it is our destiny!

So if you've been tempted to fear or to feel hopeless about the changes happening in this age, it's time for you to *deal* with the situation. Tell that fear to *leave* in Jesus' name! Then *embrace* the challenge. Ask God to help you allow His delivering power to work through you to bring freedom to people who are confused or gripped with fear. The world is looking for hope — and you have a great hope to give them!

Pray for God's Perspective

God has great plans for you. You may not see it right now. In fact, you may be going through a crisis, and it may feel like God has forgotten you. But rather than look at your crisis, ask God to open your eyes to see His *opportunity*.

Every crisis that threatens failure can also be an opportunity for great blessing and success. For example, think about how many people became rich in the tumultuous aftermath of the

Great Depression. When the financial markets crashed, the world screamed *crisis* — and it was *indeed* a crisis. But there were a few people who saw opportunity and invested against the grain of the economic wisdom of the day. Because they viewed things differently than others, they secured their future for their own generation and for generations to come.

Similarly, your ability to be fruitful and to effectively fulfill your divine call lies in whether you see your life the way God sees it. Failure doesn't have to be final, and every setback you experience doesn't mean it's the end of the road for you or your calling.

Just think for a moment about the "finality" of the Cross. When Jesus died, what do you think God saw? Do you think He had the same thoughts that others had who were saying, "Well, it's over; Jesus is dead"?

No! God didn't see it that way at all! Instead of seeing *death*, God saw *resurrection*. Instead of seeing the *end*, God saw a *beginning* for you and me. Through Jesus' death and resurrection, He saw the opportunity for mankind to be redeemed and rescued from eternal death and hell. Oh, that God would give us eyes to see life the way He sees it!

> **Your ability to be fruitful and to effectively fulfill your divine call lies in whether you see your life the way God sees it. Failure doesn't have to be final, and every setback you experience doesn't mean it's the end of the road for you or your calling.**

God wants to use you in a significant way — and your ability to be used by Him doesn't depend on your education, your money, or your status in society. It doesn't depend on where you came from. Your effectiveness in life depends only on your heart and your availability. If you'll say *yes* to God — if you'll allow Him to position you in the place He's ordained you to be and then determine to *stay* at your post, no matter what — victory *will* come to you.

I'm not telling you anything I haven't experienced firsthand in my own life and ministry. Being in the will of God — knowing His will and doing it — is the key to success in life. If you'll just do what God says to do, you'll be happy and blessed.

Think back to Aquila and Priscilla. When this couple arrived in Corinth, things looked pretty dismal in the natural. But God had a plan! The truth is, if Aquila and Priscilla had stayed in Rome, they probably never would have connected with the apostle Paul to help him pioneer churches — *or* experienced the supernatural power of God that transpired after their unexpected journey to Corinth. What the devil meant for harm in Aquila and Priscilla's lives, God turned around for their good and then used it for His glory.

And that is what God will do for you as well — IF you'll learn to see every crisis as an opportunity.

> **Even in the face of apparent defeat, God can take you places that you never imagined you could go and connect you with people He has divinely ordained for you to meet to fulfill His purposes for your life.**

As we've seen in the lives of Paul, Aquila, and Priscilla, even in the face of apparent defeat, God can take you places that you never imagined you could go and connect you with people He has divinely ordained for you to meet to fulfill His purposes for your life.

This may require an adjustment in your thinking as you learn to see yourself as God sees you. Your life is infinitely valuable — and the plan God has for you is certain and sure. So adopt the attitude: *No matter what happens or what others may do to me, I can and I WILL fulfill God's plan for my life. Since God is for me, who can successfully stand against me? God will connect me with those I need to be connected with, and His plan for me WILL be fulfilled!*

THINK ABOUT IT

1. All of us face times of crisis, and how we see and respond to them is vital. Look back over your life and describe a past crisis that God pulled you through. How did He turn your mess into a miracle? As you remember what He said to you at that time, how does that help you in light of a current situation you may be facing?

2. What opportunities do you see around you that you can use to show and share the love of God? Pray for God to open your eyes to the opportunities He has placed before you. Ask Him for a plan of action and for His grace to carry it out.

3. First Peter 3:15 instructs us to "...be ready always to give an answer to every man that asketh you a reason of the hope that is in you...." Take some time to write a brief testimony of how Jesus Christ has impacted your life — including things like what He's saved you from and how He has blessed you. Sharing with others your personal experience with Christ is powerful and useful to connect people to Him.

4. God wants you to get the word "crisis" out of your mouth and to insert "opportunity" in its place. The power of life and death is in your tongue (*see* Proverbs 18:21).

   Which of your words come to mind that you know are producing death in your life? God's will comes from His Word hidden in *your* heart and spoken from *your* mouth. The Holy Spirit will give you a *rhema* word for a specific situation — the sword of the Spirit — to cut off destructive mindsets that the enemy has sought to build into your soul through words that produce death. When you receive those Spirit-quickened words, be diligent to hide them in your heart and begin speaking them over your life.

CHAPTER ELEVEN

PASS UP EVERY OPPORTUNITY TO BE OFFENDED!

*I*n life, we all have opportunities to get upset or offended by things that happen. Part of living life victoriously is learning how to pass up those moments and refusing to allow offense to sink its stinger into our souls and negatively affect us.

I think of the enormous temptation it must have been for Aquila and Priscilla to take offense as they were evicted from their home and their city. What a grief that must have held for them! However, it appears that Aquila and Priscilla passed by that opportunity for offense — because in Corinth they were able to immediately recognize their divine connection with Paul for what it was and to follow through on it. That strategic crossing of paths was the catalyst that would move this couple upward into the next phase of ministry that God had waiting for them.

On the other hand, consider what would have happened if Aquila and Priscilla *had* become offended by that forced eviction from everything that was familiar to them. Such an offense could have derailed them at a crucial juncture in their walk with God. At that critical moment, they needed to be in close fellowship with the Holy Spirit and in position to immediately recognize a divine connection as it transpired. The couple also had to maintain their peace and remain clear in their hearts to hear His direction for the path going forward. If Aquila and Priscilla had become offended, that offense would have muddied their spiritual discernment and possibly prevented them from seizing a key opportunity to attain divine destiny and His highest and best for their lives.

Maintaining a right heart attitude is vital in the pursuit and ultimate fulfillment of God's call on your life. Think about how important your physical heart is. Although it's invisible to the natural eye, your physical body cannot live without it. The heart has a direct impact on every single part of the human body as it pumps blood through arteries and many miles of blood vessels.

> Maintaining a right heart attitude is vital in the pursuit and ultimate fulfillment of God's call on your life.

A person's natural heart is a powerful reflection of the spiritual heart, or the innermost part of a man. The natural heart pumps blood into every part of the body and thereby influences a person's ability to live and function. However, it is what is produced and entertained in a person's innermost *spiritual* being that determines the ultimate outcome of his life.

Jesus said it is what comes out of our *hearts* that defiles us (*see* Matthew 15:18-20). This is why we are instructed so strongly to "guard your heart above all else, for it determines the course of your life" (Proverbs 4:23 *NLT*).

Whatever is in our hearts is exactly what will be reproduced in our lives and conduct. We must learn to maintain a right heart attitude in order to fulfill God's will and plan for our lives.

Guard Your Heart Against Offense

Jesus said, "…It is impossible that no offenses should come…" (Luke 17:1 *NKJV*). If you are alive on the planet, you can be sure you will have an opportunity at some point in life to become offended! You will also have a choice not to give in to the temptation. Aquila and Priscilla had a prime opportunity to be offended when they were evicted from Rome and lost everything they owned. But it is evident that, by the grace of God, they chose not to give place to offense in their hearts (*see* Ephesians 4:26,27).

What is offense? The word "offense" here comes from the Greek word *skandalon*, from which we get the word *scandal*. This is a powerful picture that you must understand! The word *skandalon* originally described the small piece of wood used to keep the door of an animal trap propped open. A piece of food was placed inside the trap to lure the animal in. Once the animal entered the trap, it would accidentally bump the *skandalon*, or the small piece of wood, and cause it to collapse. The trap door would slam shut, and the animal would be caught inside with no way to escape.

That's what offense does. It slams the door shut to freedom, trapping you within the narrow confines of your negative thoughts and attitudes so you can't move forward in accomplishing God's will for your life.

An offense usually occurs when you see, hear, or experience a behavior that's so different from what you expected that it causes you to falter or wobble in your soul. In fact, you're so stunned by what you observe or experience — or by a failed expectation — that you emotionally lose your footing. You feel dumbfounded and flabbergasted. The more you think about it, your shock turns into disappointment — and then your disappointment turns into offense.

This was the opportunity of offense that was thrust on Aquila and Priscilla when they were forcefully and unexpectedly expelled from their home and lost virtually everything. The series of unexpected events they experienced were extremely difficult to live through. The couple must have been sorely tempted to falter and allow disappointment and offense to derail them. But by God's grace, they didn't give place to the offense. Instead, they maintained a right heart attitude and, as a result, positioned themselves to fulfill God's will for their lives.

DON'T ALLOW BITTERNESS TO TAKE ROOT

It's important to consider what would have happened if Aquila and Priscilla had given place to offense and become bitter and filled with resentment about their situation. As I said previously, a choice to stay offended could very well have prevented this couple from instantly connecting with the apostle Paul and keeping their divine appointment with destiny!

> A choice to stay offended could very well have prevented this couple from instantly connecting with the apostle Paul and keeping their divine appointment with destiny!

When a person becomes offended and doesn't deal with that offense correctly, those negative thoughts often churn and fester so long in a person's soul that the offense turns into a root of bitterness. This is exactly what Hebrews 12:15 is talking about when it says, "Looking diligently lest any man fail of the grace of God; lest any root of bitterness springing up trouble you, and thereby many be defiled."

The word "root" comes from the Greek word *ridzo*. It refers to *a root*, such as the root of a tree. These are roots that *have gone down deep and are now deeply embedded.* Therefore, the word *ridzo* often denotes something that is *established, deeply embedded,* or *firmly fixed.*

The words "springing up" in Hebrews 12:15 are from the Greek word *phuoo*, which depicts *a little plant that is just starting to sprout and grow.* It isn't a large plant yet; rather, it's a small seedling that is just breaking through the soil and starting to peek out at the world. However, the very fact that it's peeking through the soil means that a seed had been planted in the soil and that some kind of root system now supports the growth of that plant.

This imagery in Scripture is very significant. It tells us that bitterness doesn't overwhelm a person who harbors offense all at once. Instead, it's a toxic weed that grows gradually beneath the surface until it finally becomes a huge, ugly growth that defiles not only that person's life, but also the lives of many others with whom he or she comes in contact.

Bitterness usually begins sprouting out of the soil of our souls in the form of negative thoughts or a sour, sharp, distrusting, cynical attitude toward someone who has offended us. If the root is not quickly uprooted and removed, the bitterness will eventually become a full-blown, poisonous vine producing *bitter, wounding, hurtful,* and *scornful* fruit in the life of everyone who eats it.

> **Bitterness is a toxic weed that grows gradually beneath the surface until it finally becomes a huge, ugly growth that defiles not only that person's life, but also the lives of many others.**

If Aquila and Priscilla had held on to offense and become bitter over the persecution and pain they had endured, they would have disqualified themselves from the call of God. Instead, they dealt with their hurts and disappointments before any bitterness had an opportunity to take root.

I can only speculate what kind of conversations Aquila and Priscilla must have had between themselves as they were ordered to quickly pack a few of their belongings and abruptly leave their home, their friends, and all that was familiar to them. Were they disappointed in believers who may have stirred up problems that created a mess for the whole local Jewish population? Did they grapple with feelings of resentment toward the Emperor Claudius, since he was the one who ordered the Jews to evacuate? Did they help each other by talking it out and then prayerfully releasing to the Lord all feelings of disappointment and potential offense? All these questions reflect emotions and processes that are commonly experienced by people going through such a horrible ordeal.

If you keep your attitude right and your heart free of offense — if you'll respond in faith, love, and forgiveness — even disaster can be turned into your victory. You'll find the inner strength to step right over that obstacle and move forward with great momentum in your walk with God. What looks like a blockage in front of you can even become a steppingstone to help get you where God wants you to be.

Of course, if you nurse a wrong attitude of offense and bitterness, it will remain a blockage. And until you get serious about dealing with that wrong attitude, you'll stop right there and go no further in life.

We all have reasons to become bitter because of what we've experienced in life. But if we want God to use us, we *must* be diligent to stay free of bitterness and offense and to walk in His love toward other people.

Aquila and Priscilla undoubtedly chose to look beyond the wrong that had been done to them and to keep their hearts and their attitudes right. They evidently determined to believe that somehow, in the middle of it all, God was going to take what the devil had done and turn it around for their good (*see* Romans

8:28). As a result, the personal crisis they had just endured turned into the most glorious opportunities for ministry they had ever experienced.

This couple became part of the team that founded both the church of Corinth and later the powerful church of Ephesus. Then in the years that followed after Claudius died and his edict of expulsion was lifted, Aquila and Priscilla returned to the city of Rome, where they helped lay the foundation for the church of Rome (*see* Romans 16:3,4). An early writing also indicates that Aquila was later ordained as a leader of a church in the province of Asia.[4] Because Aquila and Priscilla responded correctly to crisis and maintained a right heart attitude, void of offense, God was able to mightily use them for many years to come.

DON'T CAST AWAY YOUR CONFIDENCE

Regardless of the difficult circumstances you may find yourself in, it is imperative that you know in your heart that if you're surrendered to God and trusting Him in your difficulty, *He is in control of your situation.* You may not emotionally feel like He's in charge, especially if things don't seem to be turning around yet. But you can be sure that God knows what is happening in your life. He has not forgotten about you. He still remembers what He promised you.

The book of Hebrews was written to a group of Jewish believers who had suffered tremendous loss of personal possessions as a result of persecution, just as Aquila and Priscilla had. For years, those Hebrew believers had believed and waited for God to bring restoration to their lives. But at the time the book of Hebrews was written, that restoration hadn't occurred yet, and the people had become disheartened. In fact, they were close to losing all hope.

---

[4]*Apostolic Constitutions,* VII.46.

The people's desperation must have been intense, because the writer of Hebrews told them, "Cast not away therefore your confidence, which hath great recompence of reward. For ye have need of patience, that, after ye have done the will of God, ye might receive the promise" (Hebrews 10:35,36).

These verses tell us that these early Christians were so weary of waiting that they were about to give up. They were suffering, and the answer to their prayers hadn't manifested yet. These believers were languishing in the "in-between time" between the prayer and the answer — which is always one of the most difficult times in which to maintain a right heart attitude.

But God knew the people were close to giving up, so He exhorted them, "Cast not away therefore your confidence...." The word "cast" comes from the Greek word *apoballo*, and it literally means *to throw away*. This word didn't depict the casual throwing away of something; rather, it was a deliberate choice to *forcefully throw the object* so far away that it would never be seen or dealt with again.

This same word, *apoballo*, is used to describe blind Bartimaeus's attempt to get up and reach Jesus. A garment was wrapped around Bartimaeus's legs, which restricted his movement. Because that garment kept him from going where he wanted to go, the Bible says he *cast away* his garment and came to Jesus. In other words, Bartimaeus grabbed hold of the garment, forcibly jerked it off his legs, and threw it out of the way (*see* Mark 10:50). Finally free of what hindered him, Bartimaeus could get up and do what he wanted to do.

I refer to this story to help you understand how the Greek word *apoballo* is used in Hebrews 10:35. These Hebrew believers had waited *and waited* for their promise from God to come to pass. They were bound by their faith to stand on the promise of God and wait for Him to work a miracle in their lives.

But apparently these believers were tempted to give up on waiting for God's promise to manifest in their lives. It seems that rather than standing strong in faith, they were tempted to harbor such thoughts as, *Why should we keep sitting around waiting for a promise that has never been fulfilled? If we cast away the promise, at least we can get up and get on with our lives. Waiting for God to fulfill His promise has kept us sitting here all these years when we could have moved on and done something else. Maybe we should just forget the Word of God and try to work out some kind of solution on our own.*

Seeing that these believers had lost heart and were tempted to quit, God had a message for them: "Cast not away therefore your confidence..." (Hebrews 10:35). In other words, *"Don't throw away your confidence as if it's a nuisance or hindrance to your life...."*

Why was the writer of Hebrews so insistent about this? Because our confidence "...hath great recompence of reward...." The word "recompense" is the same Greek word for *salary*. This means "payday" is coming — and when it comes, it will be *great*!

YOU NEED PATIENCE!

Right after God says, "Cast not away therefore your confidence...," He adds, "For ye have need of patience, that, after ye have done the will of God, ye might receive the promise" (v. 36).

Take a look at the word "patience." It is actually taken from the word *hupomeno* and would be better translated *endurance*, or as one expositor has called it, *"staying power."* It is a compound of the words *hupo* and *meno*. The word *hupo* means *under*, and the word *meno* means *to stay* or *to abide*. The word *meno* also carries the idea of *a decision to stay in one spot and not move*.

When these words are compounded, they form the Greek word *hupomeno*. This portrays the picture of a person under (*hupo*) a great load of stress and pressure who has decided to stay (*meno*) in that spot, no matter how difficult the situation.

The Early Church called this quality the *"queen of all virtues."* Early Christians believed that if they possessed the virtue of patience, they'd eventually come out on top! If they had *staying power — the power to hang in there* — the opposition would eventually let up and they'd be the winners!

This same Greek word, *hupomeno*, can also be found in James 1:3, which says, "Knowing this, that the trying of your faith *worketh patience*." We know what patience means, but what about "worketh"?

The word "worketh" is a compound of two Greek words, *kata* and *ergo*. The word *kata* carries the idea of *something that is working downward with a strong force*. The Greek word *ergo* means *to work*. When the two words are compounded, the new word formed is *katergadzomai*, which means *to work through and through* or *to work from the top to the bottom*, as a baker works yeast through a batch of dough by kneading it. In this case, James 1:3 refers to it as *patience* being kneaded and "worked through" every fiber of a person's being.

Whenever the devil comes with pressure to push you off your stance of faith regarding a difficult challenge, you have a crucial choice. You can give up and say, "Faith doesn't work." *Or* you can choose to prove your faith by determining, "I refuse to cast away my confidence and my confession of faith! God told me that this is part of my spiritual inheritance, and I'm going to have it. The Word of God is true, and I'm *not* going to back off!"

When you set yourself in that position of faith, something supernatural happens and a divine process is released. Your choice to maintain a right heart attitude and a firm confession of faith will supernaturally "work" patience into your life. Your firm choice to resist the enemy's strategy to discourage you causes God to supernaturally join you in that situation. He begins "kneading" patience, or endurance, into your heart and soul, and He doesn't stop until you are completely filled and saturated with endurance from top to bottom!

> Your choice to maintain a right heart attitude and a firm confession of faith will supernaturally "work" patience into your life.

That's why your response in the face of the enemy's attacks is so crucial. The moment you make the decision not to budge or flinch, God's *katergadzomai* process begins in you. Like a Master Baker working a batch of dough, He kneads this amazing ingredient called *hupomeno* ("endurance") all the way through your heart and soul.

Yes, it may take time for your answer to manifest. Just because your request is in accordance with God's will doesn't mean the answer will always quickly come to pass without a hitch. There's a devil out there that doesn't want you to experience God's will for your life, as we will see more clearly in the final chapter.

But Satan is ultimately powerless to stop you in your stance of faith and patience. *God's Word cannot fail!* And it will not fail *you* if you'll exercise this kind of determination. Make the decision once and for all: "Quitting is *not* an option, and I will not back down from my firm position of faith!"

TAKE YOUR POSITION!

So don't cast away your confidence when you're in a tough spot in life. Instead, make this your bold confession of faith:

"God, this is Your revealed will for my life. This is what I want, and *I'm not moving* until I receive the fulfillment of it!" As you assume this position, you trigger the process for God to work *hupomeno* (endurance) in and through your heart and soul as He works on your behalf to bring the answer to your prayer.

If the pressures of life have been closing in on you — making you think about giving up — don't do it! Open your heart to the ministry of the Holy Spirit, and ask Him to give you the endurance you need to finish the race you're running. He wants to give you *staying* power — *"hanging-in-there"* power — so you can make it all the way to the end of your course of faith.

> **Open your heart to the ministry of the Holy Spirit, and ask Him to give you the endurance you need to finish the race you're running.**

Hebrews 10:36,37 goes on to promise that if you will hang in there — holding on tight to what God has promised as you carry out His will — you will receive the things you've set your expectation on and believed to come to pass. This scripture doesn't say how quickly your answers will come to pass, but it promises they *will* manifest and they will not tarry. In other words, the answers to your prayers of faith won't be one minute late, as long as you'll hang in there and keep standing on the Word.

I want to encourage you to keep your eyes on the Lord. Focus on the answer — not on the delay! Maintain a right heart attitude full of faith and free of offense and bitterness. God is in control of your situation, and He is working on your behalf, whether or not it feels like it or you see any results. His Word is sure, and what He has promised *will* be fulfilled. So *refuse* to cast away your confidence in His faithfulness, because where your answer is concerned, it's only a matter of time!

Think About It

1. How would you describe your current heart attitude? Is your heart filled with the love, joy, and peace of God's Spirit, or is it cluttered with offense and bitterness because of disappointments with life or people? What evidence confirms your answer?

2. Are you in a state of offense? Have someone's actions or your life experience been so different from what you expected that it has caused you to trip, stumble, or lose your spiritual footing? If so, describe what happened. As an act of your will, take time now to *release that person* or *situation* into God's hands.

3. Are you dealing with a root of bitterness? Have you held on to offense so long that it has become rooted in your heart? Check your life to see if it bears evidence of any telltale signs of this sickness of the soul. For instance, when you hear a certain person's name or see his or her face, do you start feeling irritated and aggravated inside? Do you have negative thoughts and feelings about someone that just won't seem to go away? If you can identify with any of these symptoms, bitterness may have taken root. Pray and ask the Lord to show you the true state of your heart, and repent of anything He reveals that grieves Him.

4. The Word of God in the hands of His Holy Spirit is the greatest means for maintaining a pure, right heart. Be honest with yourself: How often do you presently invest time in prayer and in reading and meditating on Scripture? What can you do to increase your investment in God's presence and His Word? Pray and ask Him for fresh ideas to fill your spirit with more of Him!

CHAPTER TWELVE

DON'T YIELD TO PRESSURE TO DEVIATE FROM GOD'S PLAN

*W*hen you are faithfully serving God and doing your best to obediently fulfill His call on your life, the devil can't stand it. He will do *anything* he can to cause you to deviate from God's plan or to drop out of your spiritual race altogether.

Sometimes the enemy will use people to try to pressure you out of the will of God. If you are overly concerned or driven by what other people think of you, you can become very vulnerable in your Christian walk. Appropriately, the Scripture warns of this: "Fearing people is a dangerous trap, but trusting the Lord means safety" (Proverbs 29:25 *NLT*).

There are many ways the enemy tries to impede or derail progress when a person is giving it his best shot to fulfill God's plan for his life. In Second Corinthians 2:11, the apostle Paul clearly wrote that the devil will attempt to use many

> If you are overly concerned or driven by what other people think of you, you can become very vulnerable in your Christian walk. Appropriately, the Scripture states, "Fearing people is a dangerous trap, but trusting the Lord means safety" (Proverbs 29:25 *NLT*).

different types of "devices" against us. In that verse, Paul told us that we are not to be ignorant of those satanic tricks, nor should we be outwitted by strategies that the devil utilizes to take advantage of us.

Remember, we're the ones with the huge advantage over the enemy, because the Holy Spirit lives inside us! And as we carefully listen to His voice and obey the Word of God, we can stay on track with God's plan, no matter what the devil does to try to lure us off course.

> **Whatever situation you find yourself in, the Holy Spirit is ready, willing, and more than able to help you refocus your attention on God's plan for your life and resist all pressure to deviate from it.**

Whatever situation you find yourself in, the Holy Spirit is ready, willing, and more than able to help you refocus your attention on God's plan for your life and resist all pressure to deviate from it.

A TEST FOR PAUL

Let's again turn our attention to the apostle Paul and the lesson he learned when he was "pressed in the spirit" to reverse the order of his calling (*see* discussion of Acts 18:5 in Chapter Seven).

As a brief recap of the previous chapters, we saw that after ministering alone in Athens for a length of time, Paul arrived in Corinth. Soon after, God supernaturally gave him a divine connection with Aquila and Priscilla, and the three began working together to preach the message of salvation through Jesus Christ. It was during this time that Paul finally became more focused on reaching the Gentiles.

Meanwhile, Silas and Timothy were still in Berea. As discussed in Chapter Seven, the Christians at Berea had sent Paul away because hostile Jews from Thessalonica had come to Berea to stir up trouble for the apostle (*see* Acts 17:13,14). Time passed, and Silas and Timothy finally reconnected with Paul in Corinth.

It had been awhile since this threesome had been together. Silas and Timothy knew Paul well; they had traveled together and knew his style, his lifestyle, and his heart. But when they arrived in Corinth, it seems they quickly noticed that there was something different about Paul since they had last seen him approximately a year earlier.

When Silas and Timothy reconnected with Paul in Corinth, he was beginning to focus on a Gentile audience — and in the process, Paul was experiencing a new type of success. I personally surmise that when Silas and Timothy arrived, they were stunned by this development. It would have been logical for them to comment, "Paul, we see that you have shifted your focus. You are no longer putting your attention on the Jewish community as you have always done in the past. It seems you have changed your focus to Gentiles!"

Of course, this was a major change in Paul's behavior based on his past activities. It could have been perplexing to Silas and Timothy when they first arrived. They may have even questioned whether he had forgotten his own people. Although this is all speculation, what happened next is not speculation at all.

Acts 18:5 says, "And when Silas and Timotheus were come from Macedonia, Paul was *pressed in the spirit*, and testified to the Jews that Jesus was Christ." The word "pressed" means *to be pressured* or *to be compelled*. And as I mentioned in Chapter Seven, the older Greek manuscripts actually do not include the phrase "in the spirit." Therefore, this verse actually says that Paul suddenly felt *pressured* or *compelled* to direct his ministry to the Jews after Silas and Timothy arrived.

The Bible doesn't tell us exactly what happened, but it does say that as soon as his colleagues arrived, Paul felt "pressed" to go to the Jews. It is entirely possible that this pressure came from Silas and Timothy as they tried to convince Paul not to forget the Jewish side of his ministry. Whatever pressure Paul was feeling, it seems that he didn't experience it until Silas and Timothy arrived. And it appears as though he gave in to that pressure and turned his focus back to the Jews.

The results of Paul's preaching to the Jewish community in Corinth were the same as they had always been in every other city — chaotic, frustrating, and with a disappointing lack of fruit. These were the same results Paul had experienced in Salamis (*see* Acts 13:5) and in Antioch (*see* Acts 13:14). They were the same results he had experienced in Iconium (*see* Acts 14:1) and in Thessalonica (*see* Acts 17:1). They were the same results that took place in Berea (*see* Acts 17:10) and in Athens (*see* Acts 17:17). The results in Corinth were identical to all the previous times the apostle had put his primary focus on the Jews instead of on the Gentiles.

WHEN LOVED ONES DON'T AGREE
WITH GOD'S PLAN FOR YOU

Praise God for good friends, but we cannot let even good friends sway us from doing what we know in our heart to be God's instructions to us. We should listen to friends and family members who deeply love and care for us — and hear what they have to say. However, we can't allow even people close to us to talk us out of being where God has called us to be. *We must never yield to pressure to deviate from God's plan for our lives.* (For more on this subject, I recommend that you read my book *Dream Thieves*.)

When God first called my family to move to the USSR, not everyone close to us was thrilled or in agreement with what we were about to do. However, the people who were concerned were also people who loved us, who cared for us, and who had walked with us every step of the way. We would have been foolish not to seriously consider what they had to say about our upcoming move. Even if we didn't agree with their counsel, it was correct that we listened to them. Once Denise and I had heard every argument and opinion, it was up to us to obey what the Holy Spirit was telling us to do.

In the end, we followed the leading of the Holy Spirit, which did not always coincide with the counsel we had been given. But we profited from the conversations we'd had with friends and loved ones, and we acknowledged their deep love for us. And because we honored our loved ones in the process, we had their support in the end — *not* their voices of disagreement. Those open, candid conversations didn't negatively affect us; they actually helped us count the cost regarding what we were doing. That process helped solidify what we believed the Holy Spirit was leading us to do and strengthen our resolve to do it. Denise and I knew we could not deviate from what God had revealed to us.

You may have made the mistake of yielding to pressure from others and allowing it to divert you from the path of what God has told you to do. But it's not too late for you to make a course correction and get back on track!

The Point of No Return

Thankfully, Paul quickly recognized his mistake and focused on the people God had put in his heart. Acts 18:6 says, "…When they [the Jewish community] opposed themselves, and blasphemed, he shook his raiment, and said unto them, Your blood be upon your own heads; I am clean: from henceforth I will go unto the Gentiles."

Notice the phrase "they opposed themselves." This is a Greek term that describes *an army that opposes another force*. Like an opposing army, the Jews to whom Paul tried to minister resisted his liberating message. In fact, the Bible says, "They blasphemed." That word "blasphemed" is *blasphemeo*, which means *to curse* or *to speak dirty words*. So when Paul preached the Gospel to them, that Jewish audience got ugly!

Paul became so frustrated by the Corinthian Jews' reaction that "…he shook his raiment, and said unto them, Your blood be upon your own heads; I am clean" (v. 6). In other words, he was saying to them, "I am finished with you." Then he said, "…From henceforth I will go unto the Gentiles." The original Greek meaning of the phrase translated "from henceforth" is extremely strong and implies *from this moment forward.*

This was a major turning point in Paul's ministry!

Paul had reached *the point of no return*. Finally, he understood what he needed to do to avoid straying from his primary focus of reaching Gentiles with the Gospel.

> **Paul had reached *the point of no return*. Finally, he understood what he needed to do to avoid straying from his primary focus of reaching Gentiles with the Gospel.**

This doesn't mean Paul abandoned his desire to reach the Jewish community. Even in Ephesus, he attempted for three months to persuade the Jewish community to believe in salvation through Jesus. Later in Rome, while confined in a rented home under house arrest, the apostle called for Jewish leaders to come see him. He explained the Gospel to them, verifying it from the Scriptures, but then boldly concluded: "Be it known therefore unto you, that the salvation of God is sent unto the Gentiles, and that they will hear it" (Acts 28:28). But although Paul deeply loved his own natural people, the Gentile world was clearly his primary assignment.

You're Not Alone

Are you feeling like Paul felt at that defining moment during the early days of his ministry in Corinth? Do you feel *pressed* by others to deviate from the word God has spoken to you?

Hebrews 11 records the remarkable feats of faith done by various people who had to fight and struggle as they obeyed what God told them to do. Even though they faced great challenges in their walk of faith, they stayed with what God had told them and didn't deviate from His plan. As a result, they eventually saw His miraculous intervention in their lives. But in the process, nearly all of them endured challenges as they waited for their victory to come.

To let us know that we're not alone in our own walk of faith, the writer of Hebrews wrote, "Wherefore seeing we are compassed about with so great a cloud of witnesses, let us lay aside every weight, and the sin which doth so easily beset us, and let us run with patience the race that is set before us" (Hebrews 12:1). Notice that phrase, "…compassed about with such a great cloud of witnesses…." The phrase "compassed about" is taken from a Greek word that depicts something that is *piled high* and is *lying all around you on every side.*

Therefore, this verse carries the following ideas:

- *"Wherefore seeing we have lying all around us on every side…."*

- *"Wherefore seeing these biblical examples are piled up and lying all around us...."*

You see, the Bible is piled high with stories of people — *people just like you* — who stood in faith and endured difficulties to accomplish what God instructed them to do. You are surrounded on every side with these powerful examples — those who were challenged in their faith, yet who held on to the Word of God and didn't deviate from God's plan. And as a result, these godly people saw His promises come to pass in their lives!

You are *not* alone! Look at Noah, Abraham, Sarah, Jacob, Joseph, and Moses. Look at the fight they each endured.

Look at Gideon, Barak, Samson, Jephthah, David, Samuel, and the prophets. Look at the fight they all endured.

> **If you will determine to keep your eyes on the Lord and draw on His strength to help you stay on track, the opposing voices and challenges will eventually move out of the way, and you'll see the victory you desire.**

Take heart! Don't give up and throw in the towel! Hard times will pass. If you will determine to keep your eyes on the Lord and draw on His strength to help you stay on track, the opposing voices and challenges will eventually move out of the way, and you'll see the victory you desire.

When you're tempted to get discouraged, just remember the many examples piled up all around you of people who endured and later won their prize!

Heaven's Bleachers Are Loaded With People Like You!

The next word I want you to notice in Hebrews 12:1 is the word "cloud." It says, "…We are compassed about with such a great *cloud* of witnesses…" The word "cloud" is taken from the Greek word *nephos*. It describes *clouds* — just like the clouds you see in the sky. But the word *clouds* has an additional meaning.

In ancient, classical Greek times, the word "clouds" was used to describe *the highest seats in the bleachers of a stadium.* The seats at the very top of the stadium were called *the clouds* because they were so high up in the air. When a person went to a sports competition with a ticket for one of these seats, an usher may have said, "Your seat is in the clouds today." This meant that person would be seated in the highest row available in the bleachers.

We already know the words "compassed about" present a picture of people of faith, with their testimonies of hard-won victory piled high all around us. To make this point even stronger, the Holy Spirit uses the word "clouds." Why is this so vital? Because the Holy Spirit is emphasizing: *"You're not alone! The grandstands of Heaven all the way up to the 'clouds,' the highest seats in the bleachers, are piled high with people who stood the test of time and eventually saw their faith turned to sight!"*

As you take your own steps of faith, remember that the bleachers of Heaven are *filled* with people who faced great challenges, refused to deviate from God's plan, and eventually won. They faced the impossible; they accomplished the unthinkable; and they stand as proof that you can make it too. They're all cheering you on to victory! Just listen with the ears of faith, and you'll hear them shouting, *"Go for it! You can do it! Your faith will carry you through!"*

Lay Aside Every Unnecessary Weight

Hebrews 12:1 goes on to instruct us to "…lay aside every weight…."

What is it that keeps hindering you from fulfilling God's plan? Do you struggle with a particular sin, habit, attitude, or fear that keeps you from running your race of faith with strength, discipline, and commitment?

The words "lay aside" in Hebrews 12:1 are from the Greek word *apotithemi*, a compound of the words *apo* and *tithemi*. The word *apo* means *away*, and *tithemi* means *to place*. When the two are compounded into one word, the new word means *to remove, to lay aside*, or *to permanently put away*. It implies *a deliberate decision to make a permanent change of attitude and behavior.*

The changes we need to make will *not* occur accidentally. We must *decide* to change on purpose. We must decide *to remove, lay aside, and permanently put away* attitudes and actions that adversely affect our walk of faith.

> **What is it that keeps hindering you from fulfilling God's plan?**

Wrong attitudes and actions are so detrimental to our walk of faith that God calls them "weights." The word "weight" is from the Greek word *ogkos*, which describes a *burden* or *something so heavy and cumbersome that it impedes a runner from running his race as he should*. This "weight" is holding him back from being all he can be.

Imagine trying to run a race with hundreds of pounds on your shoulders. You wouldn't be able to run very far, would you? This is exactly what sinful habits and attitudes do to your walk with the Lord. If you don't *remove* them, they will eventually *weigh* you down and knock you out of your race of faith!

The Holy Spirit is urging us to take a good look at our lives and remove everything that weighs us down and keeps us from a life of obedience. *We must be honest with ourselves and with God.*

Do you have a bad habit or a wrong attitude that binds you? Are you plagued by a fear that weighs you down and keeps you from fulfilling your potential in Christ? Do others' negative voices and influence cause you to veer off track? Make a rock-solid, quality decision today to grab hold of those hindrances and *remove, lay aside, and permanently put them away* from your life.

Once you make that decision, God will step in by His Word and His Spirit to help you overcome. You'll find yourself running your race of faith with much more ease as you press on to victory.

CHANGE YOUR UNHEALTHY ENVIRONMENT

In addition to laying aside every weight, Hebrews 12:1 instructs us to lay aside "...the sin which doth so easily beset us...."

Your biggest potential enemy in life (besides your own wrong thinking and the devil himself) is the environment in which you live. If you constantly live in an atmosphere of doubt and unbelief, you'll have a lot more difficult time maintaining a walk of strong faith. That doubt-filled environment will eventually rub off on you!

Let me give you just one example out of many to illustrate how a wrong environment can negatively affect you. If you used to smoke or have a drinking problem, it's not a smart idea for you to hang around smokers or drinkers — *unless*, that is, you want to be influenced to return to your old habits. That environment could lure you back into those bad habits, so it's vital for you to keep yourself clear of those situations.

With this in mind, look at the phrase "…the sin which doth so easily beset us…." What kind of sin is this verse talking about? The words "so easily beset us" are from the Greek word *euperistatos*, a compound of three words: *eu, peri,* and *statos.* Let's look at all three of these words.

The word *eu* usually means *well,* but in this case, it carries the idea of *something that feels well* or *something that is comfortable.* The Greek word *peri* means *around* or *being completely surrounded.* The word *statos* is from a root word meaning *to stand.* When these three words are compounded, the new word describes *something that comfortably stands all around you, such as a comfortable environment.*

So when the Bible says, "lay aside the sin that so easily besets you," it really means *"lay aside the old, comfortable environment of sin that is surrounding you."*

> If you're not strong in your faith and you continue to live in negative, sin-filled surroundings, that old environment will begin to reach into your soul and drag you back into your old behavior again.

Sometimes in order to make necessary changes in your life, you must physically remove yourself from an unhealthy environment. If you're not strong in your faith and you continue to live in negative, sin-filled surroundings, that old environment will begin to reach into your soul and drag you back into your old behavior again.

God's admonition to lay aside every weight applies to you, so obey Him if you need to make a break from any unhealthy environment you might be in that is influencing you in a wrong way. Perhaps old friends or old places are trying to exert a bad influence on you and you're not conquering it very well. *If that's the case, get out of there!* For you, that environment is *sin* if it keeps you from fulfilling your potential in Jesus Christ.

Be honest as you consider your workplace, your friends, and your living conditions. Ask yourself, *Is this environment conducive to my walk in Christ, or is it dragging me back down into the mire I was delivered from?*

If you cannot successfully handle the environment you're in, you should remove yourself. There may be reasons why you are not able to do that at this time. In that case, ask the Holy Spirit to provide a support team to help you remain strong where you are. Seek the Lord for wisdom regarding what you can do to mitigate your involvement in that environment while you are still there. Eventually, you're going to have to take steps to remove yourself from a wrong environment — or fortify yourself where you know God has called you to be.

As you take steps to remove yourself from bad influences, you'll see God work wonders to help you along the way. He will work on your behalf as you choose to obey His leading to leave a job or distance yourself from friends who are negatively influencing you. You will see the Lord provide a better job and better friends than you've ever had before in your life.

> Your Christian life is serious business. Don't let your environment fill you with doubt and knock you out of your spiritual race.

Your Christian life is serious business. Don't let your environment fill you with doubt and knock you out of your spiritual race. If you can't handle your environment victoriously, initiate a plan of action to change it today!

YOU HAVE TO DO WHATEVER IT TAKES
TO FINISH YOUR RACE!

Hebrews 12:1 goes on to tell us, "Wherefore seeing we are compassed about with so great a cloud of witnesses, let us lay aside every weight and the sin which doth so easily beset us, and let us run with patience the race that is set before us."

God has a marvelous plan for your life that will release divine power when you get into alignment with it. That is why the devil wants to distract and divert you from fulfilling that plan. So let me ask you — do you ever feel distracted from the plan God has for your life? Do you have a hard time staying focused on your life goals? For that matter, what *are* your goals? Do you even have any? Are you running your spiritual race like a runner headed toward a finish line, or are you aimlessly running about with no sense of direction?

I want you to particularly notice the phrase "let us run" in Hebrews 12:1. The words "let us run" are taken from the Greek word that means *to run*. But this isn't the picture of a casual runner or an amateur athlete. This runner is striving to *win*! He is giving it all he's got to reach that finish line before anyone else. He is driven by *purpose*, *commitment*, and *determination*.

One of the fastest ways Satan can knock you out of your race and keep you from finishing victoriously is to get you distracted by surrounding circumstances. Any runner who takes his eyes off the finish line to look at all the commotion around him will *never* finish first. While he's looking around, others who are more focused on the finish line will pass him by and leave him in the dust. He'll end up far behind everyone else, feeling like he can never catch up or finish his own spiritual race.

If God has put a dream or vision in your heart, don't allow distractions to stop you from reaching your goal. Remember the result of the apostle Paul's pivotal moment when he decided to turn from his past pattern to embrace and focus on God's priority for his life. If voices of unbelief and adverse circumstances try to deter you from your objective, you must be like Paul in Corinth and *refuse* to let yourself get distracted and veer off course. Keep your attention focused on what *the Lord* has told you to do so you can make it all the way to the end!

Ask the Holy Spirit today to help you refocus your attention on God's plan for your life and not yield to any pressure that might tempt you to deviate from it. *He will empower you to run your race all the way to the finish line!*

> If voices of unbelief and adverse circumstances try to deter you from your objective, you must be like Paul in Corinth and *refuse* to let yourself get distracted and veer off course. Keep your attention focused on what *the Lord* has told you to do so you can make it all the way to the end!

THINK ABOUT IT

1. What are your God-given goals in life — the things you feel strongly that God has called you to accomplish? Do you know them? If not, pray and ask Him to reveal them. Once you know your goals, write down the top three. Now ask yourself: *Am I focused on running toward the fulfillment of these goals, or am I aimlessly running with no sense of direction?*

2. Hebrews 12:1 instructs us to "…lay aside every weight…." What *weight* is in your life that hinders you from living a life of obedience and fulfilling God's plan? Is it a habit, a particular sin, an attitude, or fear? Get quiet before the Lord and ask Him to show you your own heart and what things are weighing you down. Write down what He reveals, and surrender it to Him in prayer.

3. God also instructs us in Hebrews 12:1 to lay aside "…the sin which doth so easily beset us…." This is any *environment* that draws you into defeat. Pause and take an honest inventory of your surroundings — your friends, recreational hangouts, media influences, and your workplace. Are any of these luring you off the path of God's will in a direction that threatens to detour or derail your progress? Pray and ask God to reveal the truth and to give you His strength to get out of any ungodly environments.

4. What specifically has God spoken to you or impressed on your heart that you are waiting to see come to pass? How does this discussion motivate you to refuse to quit, but rather to press on? How can you use what you've learned to motivate others not to yield to pressure that would tempt them to deviate from God's plan for their lives?

CHAPTER THIRTEEN

NO MATTER WHAT THE DEVIL TRIES, GOD CAN TURN IT AROUND!

I want you to understand that the devil doesn't want you to fulfill God's will. In fact, this truth simply cannot be overstated. He is fearful of the power that will be released if you wholeheartedly obey God, and that is why He will try to stop you.

Peter described the devil "...as a roaring lion, [who] walketh about, seeking whom he may devour" (1 Peter 5:8). Jesus reveals him as "the thief [who] cometh not, but for to steal, and to kill, and to destroy..." (John 10:10). But Jesus went on to say in that verse, "...I am come that they might have life, and that they might have it more abundantly."

What a contrast! Satan is the thief who steals, kills, destroys, and devours. He is the death-bringer, but Jesus is the LIFE-giver! And the "life" He offers us comes from the Greek word *zoe*, which suggests *life that is filled with vitality*. And He offers this life "abundantly," which is from a Greek word that means *extraordinary* or even *exceeding*. It's not just *abundance* — it is *superabundance*!

It doesn't matter what the devil does — God is able to turn it around and make it work for your good. Whatever the enemy brings against you to discourage or derail you from your call, God can use it for your good as you trust Him, even though He did not authorize the assault waged against you and would never do such things to you. The Bible assures us that God "…is able to do exceeding abundantly above all that we ask or think, according to the power that worketh in us" (Ephesians 3:20).

BAD CIRCUMSTANCES ARE FROM THE DEVIL

I realize that many reading this book are facing "Goliaths" in life — difficult situations that feel like traps and seem impossible to escape. Maybe you're facing a challenge that fits that description. I certainly have experienced that feeling many times over the years. Satan actively opposes the people of God to try to keep them from fulfilling God's will. The book of James gives us some helpful insights for this particular situation.

James was writing to Jewish believers much like Aquila and Priscilla, many of whom had lost everything. They were in a ditch so deep that they didn't know how to get out of it. That ditch was dug much deeper when they began to believe that the tragedy that had befallen them was somehow allowed by the will of God. And rather than fight it, they began to think that perhaps they should just go ahead and accept it as their lot and their destiny.

These believers were thinking and believing wrong. They had begun to think that God had allowed their bad circumstances in some mysterious way and for some mysterious reason. So James set the record straight in James 1:16 and 17: "Do not err [don't think wrongly], my beloved brethren. Every good gift and every perfect gift is from above, and cometh down from the Father of lights, with whom is no variableness, neither shadow of turning."

The truth is, God is a good God who gives good things to people. He is *not* the one who sends bad things into people's lives.

This helps us know what to receive and what to reject in our lives. If we believe that the trap we're in is from God — whether it's sickness, poverty, or some other form of tragic circumstance — our time in that trap will be prolonged. Remember, *what we believe ultimately determines what we receive.*

THE DEVIL WANTS TO GET YOU OFF-TRACK

When you've been waiting to be delivered from a difficult situation for a long time, your faith in that simple truth will likely be tested. Your faith may have been strong when you started praying for God to turn things around. But as you waited and waited, and nothing changed, the devil was right there to speak to your mind. He may have bombarded you with thoughts such as, *"Maybe what you're believing is wrong. If God was going to do what you 'think' He told you He would do, He would have done it by now. You've prayed and believed. You've done everything right, but what you expected hasn't happened. Maybe you misunderstood what God wanted to do in your life. Is it time for you to let go of that dream and just accept this is the way life is going to be?"*

> God is a good God who gives good things to people. He is *not* the one who sends bad things into people's lives. This helps us know what to receive and what to reject in our lives.

The Bible says that hope deferred makes the heart sick (*see* Proverbs 13:12). The longer you wait for your answer, the more you become susceptible to discouragement. That's often when the devil tries to move in to discourage you to give up. You may begin with a white-hot faith, believing that God is a good God who does only good things. Then over a period of time, the devil begins to hit you with a variety of discouraging voices: the voice of well-meaning friends and family, the voice of experience, the voice of the doctor, the "voice" of your checkbook, and, of course, the voice of the enemy himself.

When you begin to think about the "Goliath" you are facing right now, does the devil keep saying to your mind, *"Give up, give up, give up"*? If so, don't be surprised, because the enemy wants you to let down your resistance. He wants you to abort God's plan and say, "Well, I guess I misunderstood God's will, so I'll just let go of my hopes and accept that it isn't going to happen."

That's why you must determine that you will *never* let defeat determine your theology. Don't let failure or discouragement talk you into believing that God is not going to do what He promised.

> You must determine that you will *never* let defeat determine your theology. Don't let failure or discouragement talk you into believing that God is not going to do what He promised.

Let me give you a few examples. If you are believing for your child to be healed, and he isn't healed as quickly as you want, you cannot let that affect your rock-solid conviction that God never gives sickness to people and that He has already provided redemption through His Son that includes healing from *every* disease (*see* Psalm 103:3).

Perhaps you are believing for your finances to be blessed and you are giving and doing everything right to see them turn around, but they are still in a horrible mess. You cannot let that affect what you believe about God's desire to bless you financially according to His Word (*see* 2 Corinthians 9:8)! Let me emphasize again — you must determine that you will *never* let defeat determine your theology.

So put a stake in the ground and declare, *"God keeps His Word, and He will do what He has promised. This is the truth, regardless of my present experience!"*

Every *Good* and *Perfect* Gift Is From God!

What *is* the will of God? It is expressed explicitly in James 1:17. He wants to give us *"every* good and perfect gift."

The word "good" in this verse is from a Greek word that describes something that is *good* or *beneficial*. This provides a very simple test. Just ask yourself, *Are the circumstances I'm facing beneficial?* If the answer is no, those circumstances are *not* from God because what comes from Him is *always* good and beneficial.

James took this truth even further. He said that every gift from God is "perfect." The word "perfect" is the Greek word *telos*, which describes something that *perfects, completes,* or *brings someone to full maturity.* So when God gives you something, it is not only good and beneficial, but it also *adds* to your life, helping bring you to a fuller and more complete maturity.

So you must ask yourself: "Does the situation I'm going through add to or take away from my life?" When God sends us something, it *adds* to our lives. It's really so simple. God is a good God, and the devil is a bad devil. If God does it, it's good and adds to your life. If the devil does it, it destroys and takes away from your life.

But let's go back to verse 17 for a moment. Twice in this verse, James mentioned the word "gift." In both cases, this word "gift" would be better translated, "every good *giving*" and "every perfect *giving*." This is important because it describes *something that God habitually does.* He doesn't give good and perfect gifts only on rare occasions, as many might think. On the contrary, James paints a picture of a stream of goodness continually flowing out of God to you — perfecting, completing, and maturing you.

In fact, the verse goes on to say that these gifts "come down" from the Father of lights. That phrase comes from a Greek word that carries the idea of something coming down *hard* and *continuously*, like a *downpour* of rain. That's how many good and perfect gifts God is trying to send your way. He's not doing it once a year when you've decided to behave well. He wants to literally *flood* your life with His good and perfect gifts *all the time*!

You Receive What You Believe

You might say, "If God is pouring these good and perfect gifts down on my life all the time, why am I only occasionally receiving from Him? If He is trying to bless me, why am I not being blessed?"

You have to remember that *you receive exactly what you believe.* After your obedience to align yourself fully to God's will for you, as we saw in earlier chapters concerning the life of Paul, receiving from God is all wrapped up in the exercise of your faith. Wrong believing is a trap that keeps you stuck in poverty, sickness, or other kinds of negativism. When you're bound by wrong thinking and believing, your head is down, your eyes are looking at the dirt, and you're thinking, *Oh, Lord, life is so bad. I hear what You do for other people, and it all sounds so wonderful. But why don't You rain down Your good gifts on me?*

You're not exactly in the best position to receive when your eyes are downcast and your mind is so consumed with what you *don't* have that you can't see the goodness of God pouring down on you! You have to *look up* — and this, of course, requires a decision. It's the choice that begins the process of renewing your mind to the truth of God's unchanging goodness and of His habit of giving good and perfect gifts to those who believe (*see* Romans 12:1,2).

Anytime you're caught up in negativism, it is likely that you're also stuck in the trap of wrong thinking. When you're feeling negative and downcast, you probably don't even *want* to look up. In that case, you're going to have to speak to your mind and your emotions and *make* yourself look up and start thinking differently. You will have to consciously open your mind and heart to the Word and its promises if you want to receive the goodness of God in your life.

> You're not exactly in the best position to receive when your eyes are downcast and your mind is so consumed with what you *don't* have that you can't see the goodness of God pouring down on you! You have to *look up*!

You have to take God's good gifts by faith. You have to decide to believe that they are yours because you're a child of God. You have to declare, "Every good and perfect gift is from above and is coming my way. God is pouring down His goodness on *me*!"

I beg you not to swallow the lie that your failure or your bad circumstances are from God. These are not the types of things God gives. It's time to look up, and begin to expect a literal *down-pour* of God's goodness into your situation.

Satan Will Oppose You —
But He Can't Win if You Won't Let Him

I want you to know that our decision to *cast not away our confidence, hold fast our confession of faith,* and *refuse to deviate from God's plan* will always draw a response from the devil. He *hates* a strong stance of faith. James 1:3 says that the enemy will "try" our faith. In other words, he will implement a plan of attack that is designed to convince us to give up. Satan knows that if we do give up and walk away from what God's will is for our lives, we can abort God's plan or delay it for years.

I urge you to make a firm decision today that this will never describe you!

> Our decision to *cast not away our confidence, hold fast our confession of faith,* and *refuse to deviate from God's plan* will always draw a response from the devil. He *hates* a strong stance of faith.

You may be standing your ground in faith for a manifestation of God's covenant goodness in your life, such as a healing in your body or a breakthrough in your finances. Or you may be getting ready to step out by faith into some area of business or ministry in response to the Holy Spirit's leading. Regardless, you are taking action in obedience to God's will — and that means you better be prepared for opposition from the enemy, for it will surely come.

Consider again the life of the apostle Paul. After Paul aligned himself with the primary call of God on his life to reach the Gentile world, he did extraordinary things. He started churches, raised up leaders, and shook cities with the preaching of the Gospel and the power of the Holy Spirit.

Do you think the devil wanted Paul to be doing what he was doing? Not a chance. The enemy couldn't bear the thought of Paul doing these things, so he devised a scheme to put Paul out of business.

One of the devil's strategies was to repeatedly throw Paul in prison in order to put him out of commission. With Paul in jail, the devil thought he had stopped the apostle's ministry. But as Paul sat there, the Spirit of God began to speak to his heart — and as he listened, he received some of the greatest revelation of truth he had ever received.

It was in prison that Paul had time to write inspired letters — letters that would soon become most of the epistles of the New Testament. It is entirely possible that if he had not been in prison, he wouldn't have ever written those letters because he was too busy starting churches, holding crusades, and raising up leaders. But once imprisoned, he had time on his hands and an opportunity to be still before the Lord and to write those letters, given to him by God.

Paul could have said, "It looks like my time of ministry is finished. I've been beaten; and now I'm in jail. It's all over for me." Paul could have responded that way, but he didn't. Instead, he did what we talked about in Chapter Ten — he chose to see the crisis as a new opportunity!

How we respond to crisis determines what happens next in our lives. For Paul, his place of crisis became a place of great revelation.

Paul's time of imprisonment was a strategy of the devil against him, and God had nothing to do with it. Yet the fact remains that Paul's time in prison gave him time to write those inspired epistles, which became a significant portion of the New Testament Scriptures. Paul's ministry was extended exponentially through the writing of those epistles and is still affecting our lives today, nearly 2,000 years later. The devil thought he was putting Paul

> **How we respond to crisis determines what happens next in our lives. For Paul, his place of crisis became a place of great revelation.**

out of commission, but Satan was actually putting the apostle *into position* so that he could write his epistles to the churches!

When You're Doing God's Will, Nothing Can Stop You!

In the center of God's will, you are unstoppable. It doesn't matter what the devil or life tries to throw at you, there is simply nothing and no pressure that can stop you from fulfilling God's call. That is the divine declaration in Isaiah 54:17 (*NLT*): "...No weapon turned against you will succeed. You will silence every voice raised up to accuse you. These benefits are enjoyed by the servants of the Lord; their vindication will come from me. I, the Lord, have spoken!"

When you keep yourself in the will of God, you can expect to experience supernatural provision, protection, and favor. God's power will go to work on your behalf, and you will see Him take the things the devil does to try to stop you and turn them around for your victory and His glory. Romans 8:28 (*NLT*) declares, "And we know that God causes everything to work together for the good of those who love God and are called according to his purpose for them." God will gloriously take what the devil intended for evil and make it work for your good.

The examples of Paul and of Aquila and Priscilla perfectly illustrate this point. God didn't plan all the persecution Paul suffered, nor did He plan the devastation and loss Aquila and Priscilla endured as they were evicted from Rome. But God nonetheless worked in each of their situations. Rather than let that become the end for them, God supernaturally intervened and brought these three together as an apostolic team to build His Church among the Gentiles.

God turned things around for Aquila and Priscilla — who were penniless refugees living in a pagan world — and He can turn things around for *you* too. God just needs you to dig your heels firmly into the ground of His revealed plan for your life. Determine to stay in faith, and refuse to budge from what God has shown you. As you do that, He will work in any situation — even in situations the devil thought would take you down. God will miraculously use those challenges *to lift you up* to a high place of victory!

> **God just needs you to dig your heels firmly into the ground of His revealed plan for your life. Determine to stay in faith, and refuse to budge from what God has shown you.**

You Must Be Fully and Firmly Committed and Convinced

If you know what God has called *you* to do, are you committed to keep going, regardless of what happens along the way? To stay on track with and fulfill God's plan will require a solid decision on your part. If you are going to accomplish something significant for God, you simply must decide that you will not budge from what He has spoken to your heart about your part in His plan. Because of this, I encourage you to take a serious look at your commitment level. Make sure you are *fully* committed to make it to the finish line of your divine assignment.

Spiritual toughness is essential to fulfilling what God has asked you to do. It takes guts to do His will. And if you are not totally convinced of what God has told you, the devil will throw enough obstacles in your way to derail you from the path He has laid out for your future.

If you are serious about doing the will of God, you must determine not to let anything stop you. No matter how many "hiccups" you encounter along the way, you have to set your faith and continually declare that you are *not* going to fall short of God's absolute best for your life.

If that is your constant stance of faith, you will ultimately walk away with the victory. Even more, you'll be an example to others who are believing to fulfill what God has called *them* to do. They will see that yours wasn't a flawed faith that tucked its tail and ran when things got tough. They will observe in you a faith that is genuine, unshakable, and victorious through hard times. Your example will encourage and strengthen them to stay on track in their own walks of faith and commitment.

By sticking it out through every challenge, you show who you really are in God. As a result, people will never forget those times when you stood true to your commitment, no matter what.

> **If you are serious about doing the will of God, you must determine not to let anything stop you.**

If you don't establish this kind of rock-solid commitment in your heart to make it through to the end, regardless of what comes your way, I can almost guarantee that you *won't* make it through to the end. That's why I urge you to set aside time with God and thoughtfully examine your true level of conviction to stay true to His call on your life. *Make absolutely certain that you are fully committed to do what God has told you to do!*

Where Are You in Relation to God's Will?

Maintaining a clear-cut, unambiguous, and indisputable vision is vital for your life. That trail may occasionally lead you through dense forests, dry places, and even occasional danger. But if you stay on track, the vision God placed in your heart will ultimately lead you to His destination for your life.

So let me conclude by asking you the following questions.

- Has God defined His call on your life? If so, what is it?

- Have you allowed Him to place you in the right environment to equip and prepare you for His plan?

- If the answer is yes to the first two questions, are you doing everything the Holy Spirit has prompted you to do within that right environment to prepare for your divine assignment?

Being prepared is such a vital part of doing God's will. It's a part you cannot rush or skip over. The bigger His plan, the more preparation and equipping you need.

Maybe you have already launched into doing what God has revealed as His will for your life. If that's the case, truly this is an exciting season! From here, He will begin to refine that call, just as He did with the apostle Paul. In the process, things will not always make sense to your head, but more and more, God's ways will become clearer. It was a process for Paul. It was a process for me. It will probably be a process for you too.

Sometimes in that process, you may accidentally detour from what God intended for you. But if you make that mistake — if the will of God points one way and you've gone a different way — back up to what He *last* told you. Make things right with Him, and get back on track. Be willing to say to your spouse, your family,

THE WILL OF GOD — THE KEY TO YOUR SUCCESS

your business partners, or whoever is walking alongside you in life, "We've gotten off course, and we're not going to be blessed until we get back *on* course." It might be a little humbling to admit that, but once you do and get back on the right path where God's blessings can begin to flow, everyone will thank you for being honest and willing to do whatever is necessary to fully obey the Lord!

As I've told you, when you are en route to doing God's will for your life, Satan will not stand idly by or roll out the red carpet for you to do it. But even though the enemy will oppose you, *the Holy Spirit* will help you view every crisis as a new opportunity to advance His Kingdom.

> If the will of God points one way and you've gone a different way — back up to what He *last* told you. Make things right with Him, and get back on track.

There is absolutely no impasse you cannot get through or conquer if you are really determined to achieve your God-given assignment. Don't stop until you know you've finished the job! *God is with you.* He will empower you to maintain a right heart attitude and to remain unyielding in the face of pressure that tempts you to deviate from His plan. No matter what the devil does to try to keep God's will from coming to pass in your life, *God will turn it around*!

So if finding and following the will of God has been difficult for you in the past, don't be discouraged. Set aside time to get quiet on the inside, and let the Holy Spirit show you what steps to take next. As you seek God's will for *your* life, I encourage you to follow the apostle Paul's example as he traveled the road to Corinth:

- Prayerfully reflect on your walk with God up to the present — the ways His Spirit has led you and what He has already spoken to your heart in times past.

- Ask the Lord for His wisdom, and then make this decision: *As God reveals His plan to me, step by step, I will align my own will to follow His guidance, wherever He leads.*

- Be willing to hear *whatever* God wants to say to you.

- Determine to set aside your own plans and get into alignment with *God's* plan. As you do, your obedience will bring you the greatest joy you've ever known in your life!

These are the steps that Denise and I and countless others have taken in our journeys toward finding and fulfilling God's will for our lives. We've never regretted it, and neither will you. Your life will just keep getting more exciting as you join the apostle Paul in making the unshakable commitment to "...press toward the mark for the prize of the high calling of God in Christ Jesus" (Philippians 3:14) — and never look back!

Think About It

1. Are you presently facing a problem of Goliath proportions? If so, describe the nature of your personal "giant." Have you begun to accept this situation as God's will for your life? According to James 1:13,16, and 17, why is this not true?

2. Never let defeat determine your theology. In other words, never let discouraging or debilitating circumstances define your understanding of who God is. His goodness is not measured by your present difficult experience; it is measured by His unchanging Word. How are truths like these helping you see your situation in a better light?

3. Carefully read over the original Greek meanings of the words "good and perfect gift" that we discussed in this chapter. Using these insights, write out a brief "test" you can apply to any situation or circumstance you encounter to determine whether or not it is from God.

4. *We receive what we believe.* If you've been believing wrongly and are trapped in negativity, what do you need to do to break free and start believing right? For help in answering this question, carefully read and meditate on Deuteronomy 11:18, Psalm 119:11, Romans 12:2, Ephesians 4:22-24, and Colossians 3:16. What is the Holy Spirit speaking to you in these verses?

5. It's going to take a solid commitment on your part to fulfill God's will. You must be totally convinced of what He has told you, or the devil will succeed at ousting you from your call. Take time to thoughtfully examine your level of commitment to God's call on your life. As you fellowship with Him in close, daily fellowship, ask Him for strength to do His will. Write down any adjustments or actions you believe the Holy Spirit is prompting you to act on at this time.

PRAYER TO KNOW THE WILL OF GOD

Thank you for taking time out of your life to read this book. I pray that you have been intrigued, inspired, corrected where needed, and encouraged to embrace and come fully in alignment with God's plan for your life. As we conclude, I encourage you to make this your heartfelt prayer:

Father, I come to You in the precious name of Jesus, and I ask You to give me wisdom and understanding about Your purpose for my life. You know that I've long sought to know Your plan for me and how to walk it out in full obedience.

It is the job of the Holy Spirit to help me understand the divine plan that came into my heart the moment I was born again. I am confident that this plan resides deep inside my spirit. However, I need God's plan for my life to connect with my mind so I can understand it, and I need wisdom about how to implement it. For these things to occur, that divine plan must come up from my spirit into my mind — and only the Holy Spirit can make that happen. So I ask You, Father, for this supernatural, revelatory work of the Holy Spirit to take place on my behalf. I know that You want me to understand Your unique plan for my life, so I confidently ask You for help with this today.

As I continue my journey to do what You reveal to me, give me courage and humility to admit when I've gotten off course, a heart to quickly repent, and a willingness to do whatever is required to get back on track. You are so gracious and merciful, and I know that You will help me get to where You want me to be. The plan is from You, and the power to perform it is from You, so I look to You to help me every step of the way. It's in Jesus' name I pray, *amen*!

ABOUT THE AUTHOR

RICK RENNER is a highly respected Bible teacher and leader in the international Christian community. Rick is the author of a long list of books, including the bestsellers *Dressed To Kill* and *Sparkling Gems From the Greek 1* and *2*, which have sold millions of copies worldwide. Rick's understanding of the Greek language and biblical history opens up the Scriptures in a unique way that enables readers to gain wisdom and insight while learning something brand new from the Word of God.

Rick is the founding pastor of the Moscow Good News Church. He also founded Media Mir, the first Christian television network in the former USSR that broadcasts the Gospel to countless Russian-speaking viewers around the world via multiple satellites and the Internet. He is the founder and president of RENNER Ministries, based in Tulsa, Oklahoma, and host to his TV program that is seen around the world in multiple languages. Rick leads this amazing work with his wife and lifelong ministry partner, Denise, along with the help of their sons and committed leadership team.

CONTACT RENNER MINISTRIES

For further information
about RENNER Ministries,
please contact the office nearest you,
or visit the ministry website at:
www.renner.org

**ALL USA
CORRESPONDENCE:**
RENNER Ministries
1814 W. Tacoma St.
Broken Arrow, OK 74012
(918) 496-3213
Or 1-800-RICK-593
Email: renner@renner.org
Website: www.renner.org

MOSCOW OFFICE:
RENNER Ministries
P. O. Box 789
101000, Moscow, Russia
+7 (495) 727-1470
Email: blagayavestonline@ignc.org
Website: www.ignc.org

RIGA OFFICE:
RENNER Ministries
Unijas 99
Riga LV-1084, Latvia
+371 67802150
Email: info@goodnews.lv

KIEV OFFICE:
RENNER Ministries
P. O. Box 300
01001, Kiev, Ukraine
+38 (044) 451-8315
Email: blagayavestonline@ignc.org

OXFORD OFFICE:
RENNER Ministries
Box 7, 266 Banbury Road
Oxford OX2 7DL, England
+44 1865 521024
Email: europe@renner.org

BOOKS BY RICK RENNER

Build Your Foundation*
Chosen by God*
Dream Thieves*
Dressed To Kill*
The Holy Spirit and You*
How To Keep Your Head on Straight in a World Gone Crazy*
How To Receive Answers From Heaven!*
Insights to Successful Leadership*
Last-Days Survival Guide*
A Life Ablaze*
Life in the Combat Zone*
A Light in Darkness, Volume One,
   Seven Messages to the Seven Churches series
The Love Test*
No Room for Compromise, Volume Two,
   Seven Messages to the Seven Churches series
Paid in Full*
The Point of No Return*
Repentance*
Signs You'll See Just Before Jesus Comes*
Sparkling Gems From the Greek Daily Devotional 1*
Sparkling Gems From the Greek Daily Devotional 2*
Spiritual Weapons To Defeat the Enemy*
Ten Guidelines To Help You Achieve Your Long-Awaited Promotion!*
Testing the Supernatural
365 Days of Increase
365 Days of Power
Turn Your God-Given Dreams Into Reality*
Unlikely — Our Faith-Filled Journey to the Ends of the Earth*
Why We Need the Gifts of the Spirit*
The Will of God — The Key to Your Success*
You Can Get Over It*

*Digital version available for Kindle, Nook, and iBook.
Note: Books by Rick Renner are available for purchase at:
www.renner.org

SPARKLING GEMS FROM THE GREEK 1

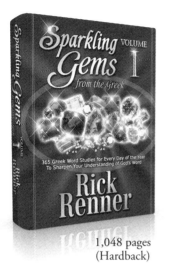

Rick Renner's *Sparkling Gems From the Greek 1* has gained widespread recognition for its unique illumination of the New Testament through more than 1,000 Greek word studies in a 365-day devotional format. *Sparkling Gems 1* remains a beloved resource that has spiritually strengthened believers worldwide. As many have testified, the wealth of truths within its pages never grows old. Year after year, *Sparkling Gems 1* continues to deepen readers' understanding of the Bible.

To order, visit us online at: **www.renner.org**

1,048 pages
(Hardback)

SPARKLING GEMS FROM THE GREEK 2

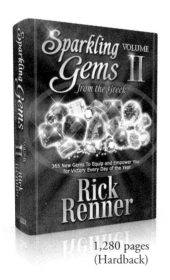

Rick infuses into *Sparkling Gems From the Greek 2* the added strength and richness of many more years of his own personal study and growth in God — expanding this devotional series to impact the reader's heart on a deeper level than ever before. This remarkable study tool helps unlock new hidden treasures from God's Word that will draw readers into an ever more passionate pursuit of Him.

To order, visit us online at: **www.renner.org**

1,280 pages
(Hardback)

DRESSED TO KILL
A BIBLICAL APPROACH
TO SPIRITUAL WARFARE AND ARMOR

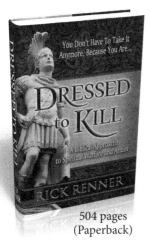

504 pages
(Paperback)

Rick Renner's book *Dressed To Kill* is considered by many to be a true classic on the subject of spiritual warfare. The original version, which sold more than 400,000 copies, is a curriculum staple in Bible schools worldwide. In this beautiful volume, you will find:

- 504 pages of reedited text in paperback

- 16 pages of full-color illustrations

- Questions at the end of each chapter to guide you into deeper study

In *Dressed To Kill*, Rick explains with exacting detail the purpose and function of each piece of Roman armor. In the process, he describes the significance of our *spiritual* armor not only to withstand the onslaughts of the enemy, but also to overturn the tendencies of the carnal mind. Furthermore, Rick delivers a clear, scriptural presentation on the biblical definition of spiritual warfare — what it is and what it is not.

When you walk with God in deliberate, continual fellowship, He will enrobe you with Himself. Armed with the knowledge of who you are in Him, you will be dressed and dangerous to the works of darkness, unflinching in the face of conflict, and fully equipped to take the offensive and gain mastery over any opposition from your spiritual foe. You don't have to accept defeat anymore once you are *dressed to kill*!

To order, visit us online at: **www.renner.org**

Book Resellers: Contact Harrison House at 800-722-6774 or visit **www.HarrisonHouse.com** for quantity discounts.

A LIGHT IN DARKNESS
VOLUME ONE

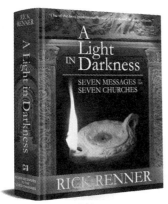

840 pages
(Hardback)

Step into the world of the First Century Church as Rick Renner creates a panoramic experience of unsurpassed detail to transport you into the ancient lands of the seven churches of Asia. Within the context of this fascinating — and, at times, shocking — historical backdrop, Rick outlines the challenges that early believers faced in taking the Gospel to a pagan world. After presenting a riveting account of the apostle John's vision of the exalted Christ, Rick leads you through an in-depth study of Jesus' messages to the churches of Ephesus and Smyrna — profoundly relevant messages that still resonate for His Church today.

Rick's richly detailed historical narrative, enhanced by classic artwork and superb photographs, will make the lands and the message of the Bible come alive to you as never before. Parallels between Roman society of the First Century and the modern world prove the current relevance of Christ's warning and instructions.

In this first volume of the *Seven Messages to the Seven Churches* series, you will discover:

- In-depth scriptural teaching that makes the New Testament come alive.

- A more than 800-page beautifully designed full-color hardback book — filled with photos shot on location, plus photos of classic artwork, artifacts, illustrations, maps, *and much more.*

- A comprehensive, completely indexed reference book.

A Light in Darkness, Volume One, is an extraordinary book that will endure and speak to generations to come. This authoritative first volume is a virtual encyclopedia of knowledge — a definitive go-to resource for any student of the Bible and a classic must-have for Christian families everywhere.

Faced with daunting challenges, the modern Church must give urgent heed to what the Holy Spirit is saying in order to be equipped for the end of this age.

To order, visit us online at: **www.renner.org**

Book Resellers: Contact Harrison House at 800-722-6774 or visit **www.HarrisonHouse.com** for quantity discounts.

NO ROOM FOR COMPROMISE
VOLUME TWO

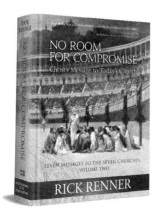

624 pages
(Hardback)

No Room for Compromise: Jesus' Message to Today's Church is *Volume Two* of the *Seven Messages to the Seven Churches* series. It presents an engaging exploration of the pagan culture of the First Century Church, with an emphasis on the city of Pergamum. Against this historical backdrop, Rick Renner highlights Jesus' message to the church of Pergamum when He appeared in a vision during the apostle John's imprisonment on the island of Patmos.

With superb photographs, many of which were shot on location in Turkey, Rick guides readers through a fascinating, detailed explanation of Jesus' message to the Pergamene church as he prophetically declares the critical significance of this message to the Church in these last days before Jesus returns. Rick also gives the reader a larger context within which to frame the pivotal moment when Jesus appeared to John on that isolated island. Rick takes the reader through a revealing overview of the first three centuries AD in which the infant Church grew amidst much opposition within a pagan world, demonstrating that darkness can never overcome the light, life, and power that the truth of Jesus Christ offers all those who believe.

Volume Two is a comprehensive, completely indexed reference book and provides:

- In-depth scriptural teaching that makes the New Testament come alive.
- Over 600 pages, including 330 beautifully designed, full-color pages.
- Nearly 400 images — including over 100 shot on location — classic artwork, artifacts, illustrations, and maps.

To order, visit us online at: **www.renner.org**

Book Resellers: Contact Harrison House at 800-722-6774 or visit **www.HarrisonHouse.com** for quantity discounts.

HOW TO KEEP YOUR HEAD ON STRAIGHT IN A WORLD GONE CRAZY

DEVELOPING DISCERNMENT FOR THESE LAST DAYS

400 pages
(Paperback)

The world is changing. In fact, it's more than changing — it has *gone crazy*.

We are living in a world where faith is questioned and sin is welcomed — where people seem to have lost their minds about what is right and wrong. It seems truth has been turned *upside down*.

In Rick Renner's book ***How To Keep Your Head on Straight in a World Gone Crazy***, he reveals the disastrous consequences of a society in spiritual and moral collapse. In this book, you'll discover what Christians need to do to stay out of the chaos and remain anchored to truth. You'll learn how to stay sensitive to the Holy Spirit, how to discern right and wrong teaching, how to be grounded in prayer, and how to be spiritually prepared for living in victory in these last days.

Leading ministers from around the world are calling this book essential for every believer. Topics include:

- Contending for the faith in the last days
- How to pray for leaders who are in error
- How to judge if a teaching is good or bad
- Seducing spirits and doctrines of demons
- How to be a good minister of Jesus Christ

To order, visit us online at: **www.renner.org**

Book Resellers: Contact Harrison House at 800-722-6774 or visit **www.HarrisonHouse.com** for quantity discounts.

LAST-DAYS SURVIVAL GUIDE

A Scriptural Handbook
To Prepare You for These Perilous Times

472 pages
(Paperback)

In his book *Last-Days Survival Guide*, Rick Renner masterfully expands on Second Timothy 3 to clearly reveal the last-days signs to expect in society as one age draws to a close before another age begins.

Rick also thoroughly explains how not to just *survive* the times, but to *thrive* in the midst of them. God wants you as a believer to be equipped — *outfitted* — to withstand end-time storms, to navigate wind-tossed seas, and to sail with His grace and power to fulfill your divine destiny on earth!

If you're concerned about what you're witnessing in society today — and even in certain sectors of the Church — the answers you need in order to keep your gaze focused on Christ and maintain your victory are in this book!

To order, visit us online at: **www.renner.org**

Book Resellers: Contact Harrison House at 800-722-6774 or visit **www.HarrisonHouse.com** for quantity discounts.

BUILD YOUR FOUNDATION

Six Must-Have Beliefs for Constructing an Unshakable Christian Life

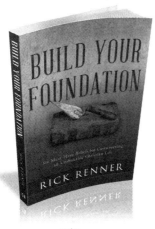

248 pages
(Paperback)

A building contractor has a top priority every time he begins a construction project: *to get the foundation right.* He knows that's the key to the stability of the structure he is building. If the foundation is laid incorrectly, the rest of the building might look good — but it will always have problems and will possibly never fulfill its purpose for being constructed in the first place.

That same principle is true as you build your life in Christ. You will never last long in your quest to fulfill what God has put you on the earth to accomplish *unless* you first focus on laying your spiritual foundation *"rock-solid"* on the truths of His Word.

In this book, author Rick Renner provides the scriptural "mortar and brick" that defines the six fundamental doctrines listed in Hebrews 6:1 and 2 — the exact ingredients you need to lay a solid foundation for the structure called your life in Christ.

Topics include:

- An Honest Look at the Modern Church
- Let's Qualify To *'Go On'*
- Remorse vs. Repentance
- The Laying on of Hands
- Three Baptisms and Three Resurrections
- The Great White Throne Judgment
- The Judgment Seat of Christ
- *And many more!*

To order, visit us online at: **www.renner.org**

Book Resellers: Contact Harrison House at 800-722-6774 or visit **www.HarrisonHouse.com** for quantity discounts.

UNLIKELY

OUR FAITH-FILLED JOURNEY TO THE ENDS OF THE EARTH

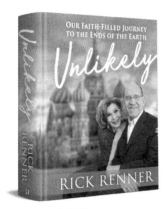

1,090 pages
(Hardback)

Rick Renner shares his life story in detail in his autobiography ***Unlikely — Our Faith-Filled Journey to the Ends of the Earth***. In this book, you'll see how our smallest decisions can lead to something *big* if we'll determine to stay the course and follow God's plan for our lives wholeheartedly.

Rick and Denise Renner's lives are "proof positive" that this is true. From their humble upbringings in small Oklahoma towns, a lack of understanding from their peers growing up, and evil assaults from the enemy that threatened to undermine God's plan, the Lord drew Rick and Denise together and sent them, with their three young sons, to live in the former Soviet Union. Rick and Denise live and minister powerfully in the former USSR to this day — and not one of their hurtful, *harrowing* experiences was wasted!

You'll enjoy reading about Rick's adventures of flying in unsafe planes across 11 time zones in the former USSR, of circumventing criminal opportunists, and of dealing with deficits of food, fuel, and heat during harsh winters just after the fall of the Iron Curtain. Rick and his family were gloriously, and, at times, *hilariously* delivered so they could deliver the message of restoration and hope God sent them to give.

You have an unlikely story too. Life is not a game of chance. It can be a thrilling adventure when you give God your *yes* and "buckle up" to receive Heaven's directive for your life. This book can show you how!

To order, visit us online at: **www.renner.org**

Book Resellers: Contact Harrison House at 800-722-6774
or visit **www.HarrisonHouse.com** for quantity discounts.

The Harrison House Vision

Proclaiming the truth and the power

of the Gospel of Jesus Christ with excellence.

Challenging Christians

to live victoriously,

grow spiritually,

know God intimately.

Connect with us on

f Facebook @ **HarrisonHousePublishers**

and ⦿ Instagram @ **HarrisonHousePublishing**

so you can stay up to date with news

about our books and our authors.

Visit us at **www.harrisonhouse.com**

for a complete product listing as well as

monthly specials for wholesale distribution.